The Gay Baby Boom

The Gay Baby Boom

The Psychology of Gay Parenthood

SUZANNE M. JOHNSON

and

ELIZABETH O'CONNOR

NEW YORK UNIVERSITY PRESS

New York and London

NEW YORK UNIVERSITY PRESS
New York and London

Library of Congress Cataloging-in-Publication Data
Johnson, Suzanne M., 1961–
The gay baby boom : the psychology of gay parenthood /
Suzanne M. Johnson and Elizabeth O'Connor
p. cm.
Includes bibliographical references and index.
ISBN 0–8147–4260–2 (cloth : alk. paper) —
ISBN 0–8147–4261–0 (pbk : alk. paper)
1. Gay parents   2. Children of gay parents—Psychology.
3. Parenting.   4. Parent and child.
I. O'Connor, Elizabeth 1961–   II. Title.
HQ75.27 .J64 2002
306.85—dc21   2001005444

New York University Press books are printed on acid-free paper,
and their binding materials are chosen for strength and durability.

Manufactured in the United States of America
10 9 8 7 6 5 4 3 2 1

We dedicate this book to
Bailey Suzanne Johnson O'Connor
and Rowan Morgan Johnson O'Connor,
our daughters.

Contents

Acknowledgments

There are a number of people whose contributions to this book we wish to acknowledge. We are especially indebted to Nanette Silverman, our research assistant, who provided invaluable help at every stage of this project. We are also grateful to Kelly Taylor, who as editor of *Alternative Family* magazine was instrumental in helping us contact participants. Suzanne's colleagues at Dowling College provided her with release time to work on this project.

Our editor at New York University Press, Jennifer Hammer, has given us thoughtful suggestions and perceptive comments on the manuscript. We also appreciate the comments of an anonymous reviewer at an early stage of this project.

We are most grateful, though, to the parents who participated in our research project. Their willingness to give of their time to tell us about their experiences as gay or lesbian parents has humbled us, and their openness is what enabled us to write this book. We hope that they feel their efforts were worthwhile.

Finally, we wish to thank our daughters, Bailey Suzanne Johnson O'Connor and Rowan Morgan Johnson O'Connor, for their patience, enthusiasm, and constant inspiration.

Introduction

The gay and lesbian community is experiencing a baby boom. Advances in gay rights, coupled with increased availability of alternative reproduction techniques and liberalization of legal restraints, have led to an unprecedented increase in the number of openly gay and lesbian parents. Estimates are that between six and fourteen million children in the United States are being raised by at least one parent who is gay or lesbian. Yet, very little is known about how gay- or lesbian-headed families function or whether they differ in any relevant ways from families headed by straight parents. Until very recently, researchers focused on different concerns.

Approaches to understanding homosexuality by mental health professionals have undergone great changes in the past several decades. It was only in 1973 that homosexuality was removed from the list of mental disorders by the American Psychiatric Association. The American Psychological Association followed suit in 1975. Prior to that time, homosexuality was viewed as a disorder. Once that view of homosexuality changed, clinicians focused on facilitating acceptance and adjustment for their gay or lesbian clients. A similar evolution occurred in the world of psychological research as researchers began looking at different aspects of gay and lesbian lives.

Advances in civil rights for gays and lesbians have accompanied these changes. Illustrating this point is the growing number of openly gay and lesbian parents. Of course, there have always been gay and lesbian parents; what has changed is their willingness to be open about their sexuality and their unwillingness to see their sexual orientation as an obstacle to having a family. This increase has been facilitated by advances in reproductive technologies and by changes in adoption laws and societal attitudes.

Concomitant with this increased openness has been an increase in the amount of psychological research undertaken on gay- and lesbian-headed families. For nearly three decades now, researchers have focused on child development outcomes in cases where a child had a gay or lesbian parent. Research on gay and lesbian families, which almost inevitably means research on the children raised in these families, is usually undertaken with no greater purpose than to find out whether the children are normal. In light of past and current prejudices and misconceptions about gay and lesbian families, this is a necessary and valuable undertaking. For example, there are very practical concerns about the treatment of these families by the legal system. Child custody cases involving gay and lesbian parents have been brought into court, and judges have been in need of information about children in these families. Judges often have questions such as "How do children raised by gay or lesbian parents fare? Are they subjected to ridicule and ostracism by their peers? Are they destined to grow up to be homosexual, too?"

Psychologists have endeavored to answer these questions. In recent years, a number of states have passed legislation on issues such as second-parent adoptions, which allows a same-sex partner to adopt the biological parent's child. Psychological research has informed those decisions. In addition, high-profile cases such as the 2000 Supreme Court case involving the Boy Scouts of America and their desire to reject homosexuals from membership have brought public attention to the convergence of homosexuality, children, and families. Psychological research has again contributed to these cases.

Demonstrating that children raised by gay or lesbian parents are as well adjusted, intelligent, and socially competent as children raised by heterosexual parents is important work, and this work can be used to bolster legal arguments and official positions. At this point, however, it can safely be said that the question of whether the children are "normal" has been answered: They are. The danger now lies in continuing to do research within this framework. What began as a necessary research methodology—the study of children raised by gays or lesbians to see if they are normal—may, ironically, lend credence to the idea that the children must not be normal. Continuing this type of psychological research can imply that there must be an increased risk of child adjustment problem in families with a gay or lesbian parent and that gay or lesbian parents are somehow deficient in their ability to raise a child to be emotionally healthy.

This does not mean that psychology need no longer concern itself with studying gay and lesbian families. Rather, it is time to refocus and reorient our research. We know that children raised in these families are not at risk for serious problems as a result of their parents' sexual orientation. What we do not know is what life is like inside the gay or lesbian family. In fact, it could be argued that, given the homophobic attitudes that still exist in our society, there must be some remarkable strengths in these families that make the children resilient enough to avoid emotional difficulties.

There has been an inherent assumption that gay- and lesbian-headed families must be different from heterosexual-headed families. Yet, the research that has focused on child outcomes has not addressed how gay and lesbian parents are presumed to differ from heterosexual parents, other than the obvious difference of gender of the parents. Generally speaking, differences in child outcomes suggest differences in family functioning. The fact that no differences in child outcome have been found between children raised by gay or lesbian parents and those raised by heterosexual parents may suggest that homosexual and heterosexual parents are more similar than they are different in both child rearing and family functioning. But, up until this point, few studies have looked inside gay and lesbian families to explore this. Do gay men bring different values and philosophies to their parenting than do lesbians? How do gay and lesbian parents cope with the challenges of living outside the mainstream? Are they more likely to talk to their children about issues such as sexuality and discrimination than are heterosexual parents? Do the obstacles to becoming parents that gays and lesbians face make them more committed to their role as parent? So far, very little is known about family functioning in gay and lesbian families.

Beyond these unanswered questions, there are additional reasons for studying gay and lesbian families. This is not a monolithic group. It encompasses gay fathers, lesbian mothers, families formed after divorce, families whose children were conceived through new reproductive technologies, adoptive families, blended families, single parents, and families with three or more parents. Differences among these types of families have so far not garnered much attention, but they should.

Given the different types of families who fit into the broad category of gay or lesbian family, it seems likely that there are significant differences among gay- and lesbian-headed families. For example, children who are born into a gay or lesbian relationship have life experiences different from those of children who live much of their lives with heterosexual parents and then have a parent begin a homosexual relationship later in life. Perhaps gay men approach child rearing differently way from lesbians. These are questions that are just beginning to be studied.

The study of gay- and lesbian-headed families can also contribute to broader theoretical work within developmental psychology. Psychologists can look to gay and lesbian families to help clarify unanswered questions that apply to all children. For example, researchers interested in children's acquisition of gender roles or the process by which children learn how males and females behave in their culture have often focused on the relative contribution of mother and father within the family. By studying the same phenomenon in families that have two mothers or two fathers, researchers can shed light on the processes involved in all families. Researchers interested in the division of labor between parents can look to same-sex parents to discover if they divide the household and childcare tasks along traditional lines, as do most heterosexual couples, or whether they find a different way of handling the work. From a methodological point of view, gay and lesbian families provide a sort of "natural experiment," and researchers are beginning to study them from this perspective. Research on gay and lesbian families need not be restricted to those who are interested in such families per se; these families can help shed light on normative developmental processes.

This book is divided into two sections. The first takes a look at psychological studies that have focused on gay and lesbian families. We review the studies that have asked, in one way or another, whether the children are normal, focusing on issues such as their intelligence, psychological adjustment, sex-role and gender-role development, and moral development and on the sexual orientation of adult children raised by gays and lesbians. We have tried to be as comprehensive as possible in presenting research conducted from the 1970s to the present. More recent studies have begun to look at family functioning within gay and lesbian families, and we provide an overview of these, as well.

Intriguing questions emerge from this literature, many of which are also relevant to other types of families. The research includes studies of parents whose children were conceived through artificial reproduction technologies. Do parents without biological ties to their children feel differently about, or behave differently with, their children? If the children are adopted, how do parents and children come to terms with the fact that there exists somewhere a biological parent who desires no relationship with the child? How do gender roles and sexual identity unfold in boys raised solely by their mothers or in girls raised solely by their fathers?

In this section, we also discuss the difficulties inherent in studying this population. Gay and lesbian parents are not as easy to locate in large numbers as are heterosexual parents. While many are eager to participate in psychological research, often they are also understandably wary about opening up about their families to people whose motivations are unclear. As a result, many studies have been plagued by small sample size.

Methodological confounds are also common. Often, children of gays or lesbians are also children whose parents have gone through a divorce. It can be difficult to tease apart the effects of a parental divorce from the effects of having a gay or lesbian parent. Finally, a bias exists, with many more studies focusing on lesbian mothers than on gay fathers. We consider the implications of these limitations.

The second section of the book is an extensive discussion of our large-scale research project, *The National Study of Gay and Lesbian Parents*, undertaken from 1999 to 2000. This study is currently the largest national assessment of families headed by people who identify themselves as gay or lesbian. Questionnaire data were collected from 415 parents, representing 256 families from thirty-four states and the District of Columbia—the largest national sample to date. We obtained data from seventy-nine gay fathers and 336 lesbian mothers. All subjects were parenting at least one child under the age of eighteen at the time of their participation.

Participants completed both quantitative and qualitative measures. These asked about their experiences as gay or lesbian parents; their concerns; their perceived areas of strength as parents; their openness in the community; their parenting philosophies and child-rearing practices; and, for those subjects in two-parent households, their adult relationship; their division of labor; and their feelings about their partner as a parent. This information enabled us to explore how gay and lesbian parents view their own family functioning and dynamics and how they view their family's experience within their community. The size of the sample allows for comparisons among different groups of gay and lesbian parents, which is rarely done, as well as for general statements about this population, both regionally and nationally in the United States. In many ways, this work moves beyond the limitations of previous research and broadens the focus of study used with gay- and lesbian-headed families.

This study is not meant to be the final word on the study of gay and lesbian parents. It is, however, the first of its size to ask these parents themselves about their family lives. We hope that it will serve as a springboard for future studies focused on gay and lesbian families. It marks a significant change in perspective and orientation, beginning to address the very same questions that have been asked about heterosexually headed families for decades. What values do parents want to instill in their children? How do parents balance their child-rearing tasks with all the other demands on their time? How well do parents work together? Are some family constellations more prone to problems than others? How do parents approach child rearing? What are their hopes and dreams for their children?

In summary, this book attempts to address two issues with regard to psychological research on gay and lesbian families: How far has the research come? And where does it need to go?

[PART ONE]

[1]

Ask the Experts

What Makes a Good Parent?

Developmental psychology studies the processes involved in children's development, encompassing many areas, including cognitive development, language acquisition, sensation and perception, social relations, self-concept, moral development, and childhood psychopathology. Developmental psychology also examines family dynamics and their associations with different child outcomes. There are different theoretical approaches within developmental psychology, which have varied assumptions about human nature and diverse areas of focus. We limit our focus to the question "What makes a good parent?," concentrating on the areas of social development and family dynamics.

Attachment Theory

Attachment theory concerns itself with the effect of early parent-child relationships on later personality and social relations.

There is a large body of research that supports the notion that the quality of children's early attachment to their parents is related to their subsequent emotional and social development (Bowlby, 1969, 1973; Main, Kaplan, & Cassidy, 1985). All infants become attached to their caregivers; what differs is the quality of that attachment. Securely attached babies are those whose caregivers have been responsive in a positive, warm fashion. Within infancy, which includes the first two years of life, being responsive has been defined as being sensitive to the infant's needs, being available for interaction, accepting the infant's attempts to interact, and being part of the infant's activities and routines.

Parents who are consistently sensitive, available, accepting, and cooperative throughout their child's first year of life tend to produce a child who has a feeling of security about the parent. This secure attachment means that the child has a sense of confidence that the parent will be there to share exciting things or will be available in times of unhappiness or distress. This confidence is formed through the many months of predictable and consistent interactions the infant has with the person or people who have consistently cared for him. It allows the child to go out and explore the world around him, to try new things, and to take risks, always knowing that, if he finds something new or needs help, his parent will be there.

Babies who are insecurely attached have caregivers who are less in tune with their signals, and respond awkwardly, insensitively, or intrusively (Ainsworth, Blehar, Waters, & Wall, 1978; Belsky, Rovine, & Taylor, 1984). These babies are not as adept at independently exploring their environment because they are less sure that they can count on their parents to provide help if they need it. Insecurely attached infants are less likely to go to their parents for comfort and less likely to be soothed if they do go to them.

According to attachment theory, children and adults form internal working models based on their attachment experiences. These models represent themselves, caregivers, and relationships, and are used to predict and interpret other people's behavior (Bretherton, 1990). In other words, people with a history of secure attachment think of themselves as lovable and expect that their relationships with others will be fulfilling. Those with a history of insecure attachments think they are not worthy of love, expect inconsistent or insensitive treatment from others, and do not expect relationships to be fulfilling. A number of research findings have been consistent with this view. In a follow-up study of children at age four who had first been studied as infants, those children who had been securely attached were more socially competent and more popular and had higher self-esteem than were children who had been classified as insecurely attached (Elicker, Englund, & Sroufe, 1992). At age eleven, children who had been securely attached as infants had better peer relationships and were seen by adults as being more socially adept (Shulman, Elicker, & Sroufe, 1994).

To a psychologist who works with attachment issues, a good parent is one who is sensitive, warm, and responsive to his or her child. This type of parental behavior allows the child to grow up with a feeling of security about himself and his place in the world. On the basis of the first relationship the child has—with his parents—he develops an idea that other close relationships in his life will be just as rewarding.

Parenting Styles

Developmental psychologists have examined different types of parenting styles to see which is most effective. When psychologists refer to parenting styles, they are talking about the ways in which parents socialize their children, that is, the ways they teach them right from wrong, encourage mature behavior, and generally handle discipline. A useful way of looking at the different ways that parents handle this issue has been to classify parenting styles along two dimensions: responsiveness and demandingness (Baumrind, 1967, 1971, 1991) Parents are either high or low on these two dimensions, resulting in four groups of parenting styles.

Authoritative parents are high on both responsiveness and demandingness. They are accepting of their children's feelings and viewpoints, openly show warmth and affection to them, and encourage their children to express themselves. At the same time, they have high standards for their children and insist that their children try to meet those standards. Their demands are reasonable, given the child's age and ability, and are clearly explained. Numerous studies have shown that children with authoritative parents do very well. They are more socially mature, have higher self-esteem and greater self-control, and achieve more educationally (Baumrind & Black, 1967; Block, 1971; Denham, Renwick, & Holt, 1991; Steinberg, Lamborn, Dornbusch, & Darling, 1992).

Authoritarian parents are high on demandingness and low on responsiveness. Like authoritative parents, they have high expectations for their children's behaviors. They differ from the authoritative parents in that they are not receptive to listening to their children's point of view. Their approach can be characterized as "Do it because I say so." They tend to tell the children what the rules are, rather than discussing the rules with them. Disobedience is met with force and punishment. Children raised by authoritarian parents tend to be withdrawn and anxious with their peers; adolescents tend to be less well adjusted than those with authoritative parents (Baumrind, 1967, 1971; Steinberg, Lamborn, Dornbusch & Darling, 1992).

Parents high in responsiveness and low in demandingness are known as permissive parents. These parents are very nurturing and accepting of their children but have few rules or expectations for them. There are very few household rules, and children are not encouraged to assume any responsibilities for themselves. Some of these parents believe that children will develop best if allowed to go at their own pace, with few restrictions on their behavior; others simply lack parenting skills. Children raised by permissive parents tend to be very immature, impulsive, and rebellious when demands are placed on them. Adolescents who are raised permissively show higher rates of drug use and are less involved in school (Baumrind, 1967; Lamborn, Mounts, Steinberg, & Dornbusch, 1991).

Uninvolved parents are those who are low on both responsiveness and demandingness. At the extreme, these parents are actually neglectful, which is a form of child abuse. At a lesser extreme, uninvolved parents show little engagement with or interest in their children and put little or no effort into establishing routines or guidelines for their children's behavior. Uninvolved parenting can lead to problems in attachment. Children with uninvolved parents tend to be demanding and noncompliant, have a low threshold for frustrations, and are more likely to engage in delinquent activity (Lamborn et al., 1991; Pulkkinen, 1982).

From the perspective of parenting styles and child outcomes, the best parent is one who is authoritative in his or her approach. This parent is physically affectionate with the child and encourages open communication with the child. The parent sets firm, fair, and reasonable goals for the child. If the goals are not met, the parent responds with a clear, rational use of control. The parent helps the child assume an increasing amount of control and responsibility for his own behavior.

Marital Relationship

The quality of the relationship between parents can have a profound impact upon their children's behavior. It is well known that a discordant marriage is a risk factor for emotional and behavioral problems in children (see Buehler, Krishnakumar, Stone, Gerard, & Pemberton, 1997, for a discussion). Several explanations have been advanced for this association. One is that parents in stressful marriages are less patient with and more critical of their children, and there is some evidence to support this notion. For example, in marriages that are marked by tension and hostility, parents are more likely to punish and criticize their children. In contrast, when parents have a warm and positive relationship with each other, they praise their children more often and nag and scold them less often (Cox, Owen, Henderson, & Lewis, 1989; Howes & Markman, 1989).

Another hypothesis is that children's perceptions about the parental conflict (whether the conflict is seen as a likely threat to them, to their parents, or to their family) and their tendency to blame themselves are the factors that mediate between parental conflict and children's behavior problems. Some evidence also exists to support this theory (Grych, Fincham, Jouriles, & McDonald, 2000). Belsky (1984) proposes that the quality of the marital relationship is more powerful than any other type of social support in either undermining or promoting effective parenting.

What may be even more important than general marital discord, in terms of child behavior, is parental disagreement about child-rearing issues. If parents are in a relatively discordant marriage, with a high level of conflict, yet agree with each other on their child-rearing philosophy and support each other in their parenting activities, the risk that the child will develop problem behavior is greatly reduced. On the other hand, if parents in a well-functioning marriage have strong disagreements about how to handle their children, the child is likely to experience inconsistent parenting, which can itself lead to problems. A strong alliance between parents on child rearing is thought to be necessary for optimal child development. In fact, Block, Block, & Morrison (1981) found that parental disagreement about child rearing is associated with problematic child behavior in school. Fauber, Forehand, Thomas, & Wierson (1990) suggest that it is not marital conflict per se that leads to children's maladjustment; rather, it is the disruption of parenting that is caused by marital conflict that leads to children's behavioral problems.

In two-parent families, optimal parenting exists when marital conflict is low and marital satisfaction is high. Parents whose relationship is harmonious and mutually supportive are in the best circumstance for effective parenting. The strength of the parental alliance should ideally be high. That is, both parents should feel strongly and positively about their partner's ability as a parent. They should show a strong commitment to parenting and agree with each other on their goals and how to achieve them.

Division of Labor

In heterosexual couples, women do the bulk of the work involved in maintaining a household and caring for the children (Chan, Brooks, Raboy, & Patterson, 1998; Cowan & Cowan, 1992; Hochschild, 1989). A traditional approach to allocating household and childcare responsibilities, with the woman assuming the lion's share of work in both areas, has not been found to result in the best outcome for parents or children. Studies of heterosexual couples with children have found that children fare better when their fathers are more involved in taking care of them (Radin, 1981). An egalitarian approach to child rearing is related to greater academic achievement for girls (Updegraff, McHale, & Crouter, 1996) and to greater marital satisfaction for both husbands and wives (McHale & Crouter, 1992). Thus, an optimal arrangement for both parents and children appears to be a relatively egalitarian approach to dividing up the family work roles. In families with two parents, having both parents equally involved in the household duties and, particularly, the child rearing responsibilities is the arrangement most likely to lead to good outcomes for all concerned.

Stress and Support

The quality of a parent's caregiving is itself related to a number of factors. Stress, for example, has been shown to adversely affect parenting. However, studies have shown that in families with high levels of stress, good social support, a good marital relationship, and a spouse's active participation in childcare can all lead to reduced stress and greater attachment security (Howes & Markman, 1989; Pianta, Sroufe, & Egeland, 1989).

Low levels of stress, or the presence of strong social and emotional support in cases where there are high levels of stress, are thus essential for optimal parenting.

Contexts of Development

Developmental psychology has become increasingly aware that families exist within a multilayered social milieu. Bronfenbrenner (1979, 1989) has characterized the child's environment as a series of systems or contexts in which development takes place. The closer the context is to the child, the more influential. Bronfenbrenner's model consists of four general contexts: beginning with the closest, they are microsystem, the mesosystem, the exosystem, and the macrosystem.

The microsystem refers to the child's immediate surroundings and includes the child's genetic makeup and biological predispositions. It also encompasses the people in the child's immediate environment, including not only parents and siblings but also extended family, the neighborhood, and school.

The mesosystem refers to the connections among the different microsystems. So, for example, child development is enhanced by communication between parents and teachers, or parents and daycare workers. The exosystem consists of social entities that do not themselves include children but that nevertheless have an impact on them. Examples of informal exosystems include the parents' social network and community ties. The parents' place of employment, which through its policies on family leave or medical insurance can help or hinder a parent, is another example.

Finally, the macrosystem, the broadest level in Bronfenbrenner's theory, incorporates the values, laws, and customs of a culture. A particular culture can establish regulations that either help families (for example, by mandating family leave to enable parents to care for a newborn or newly adopted child) or hinder them, for example, by not providing affordable, high-quality daycare.

This vast social milieu is a dynamic, constantly changing system, with influences running in all directions. In an ideal world, parents would not only provide their children with positive, responsive care but do so within the context of a supportive social network, open communication between parents and the other people in the child's life, and a larger society that values families and their parenting role.

Summary

Not all of the variables associated with good parenting are within the parent's control. Outside stress, lack of support, and societal structures that make life more difficult are facts of life for some families. However, the dynamics within a given family are much more within the control of the parents, and it is those dynamics that are most responsible for good child outcomes. None of the parental attributes or behaviors associated with optimal child outcome is dependent upon the gender or sexuality of the parents. There is no reason to believe that two men can't be responsive and accepting of a child's need or that a lesbian will be unable to be an authoritative parent. Most potential difficulties in this respect lie outside the family. Disapproval or lack of support from family, friends, and members of the community can lead to stress, increased marital difficulties, and, ultimately, problems in parenting. Gay and lesbian families are certainly at risk for encountering a lack of support from others; their families may not be legally or officially recognized, for example. In some states, a child cannot legally have two parents of the same gender. It is this lack of validation that has the potential to be harmful, not the gender or sexuality of the parents themselves.

[2]

The (Nonbiological) Ties That Bind

Gay and lesbian families include at least one, if not two, nonbiological parents. Of course, gay and lesbian families are not the only types of families of which this can be said. Adoptive families and families that have been created via assisted reproductive techniques such as donor insemination are other examples. Stepfamilies also have one parent who is not biologically related to the children. Stepfamilies face more issues than just this lack of a biological tie, however. A step-parent joins an already established family. The child has already gone through the stress of a divorce or parental death and now must go through another adjustment as a new family is created. How parents in these situations cope with not being biologically related to their children, and the effects on the children, has received a significant amount of scholarly attention over the years.

Assisted Reproduction

The world's first "test-tube" baby was born in 1978, garnering worldwide attention. Since that time, advances in assisted reproduction have been astounding. While the "test-tube" baby was conceived via in vitro fertilization (IVF) using her mother's egg and her father's sperm, it has become more common for infertile couples to use donor sperm or donor eggs. Current estimates are that somewhere between thirty-thousand and fifty- thousand children are conceived each year in North America using donor insemination (DI). While it is becoming more common for single women and lesbians to use DI to become pregnant, the technique has most often been used in heterosexual couples where the male is infertile.

An issue that has been of great concern to psychologists who study heterosexual couples who have conceived via DI is whether it is best that the child be told that her father did not play a role in her conception. For a long time, clinicians counseled parents that it was not in the child's best interest to be told of the circumstances of her conception (see Mahlstedt & Greenfield, 1989, for example). More recent lines of thought have suggested that keeping secrets is ultimately detrimental to the parent-child relationship and that the lack of information about the donor may be harmful (see Snowden, 1990). Children conceived in this manner may at some point wish or even need to have more information regarding their donor's medical history (Nachtigall, 1993). There is still controversy in the area. Some parents who conceived using DI do not choose to disclose this information to the child or to anyone else because of a desire to protect the child's feelings, embarrassment over the father's infertility, or fear of disapproval from others (see Bernstein, 1994; Pruett, 1992; Vercollone, Moss, & Moss, 1997).

For gay or lesbian couples who have conceived using any form of reproductive technology, the issue of whether to disclose this fact to the child does not arise. Whereas a child with two heterosexual parents would have no reason to suspect that they are not her biological parents, a child with two mothers or two fathers, or a single parent, will recognize quite early on that someone else must have played a role in her conception. There is thus no issue of secrecy among gay and lesbian parents. The question that remains is whether one parent's lack of a biological tie to a child per se impacts upon the parent-child relationship.

A number of studies have compared family functioning and the parent-child relationship in families that were created using assisted reproduction techniques and those whose children were naturally conceived. Golombok, Cook, Bish, & Murray (1995) examined functioning in four groups of British families: forty-one who conceived a child by IVF, forty-five who conceived using DI, fifty-five who adopted an infant in the first six months of life; and forty-three with a naturally conceived child. The children were between the ages of four and eight at the time of the study. The researchers found that the quality of parenting in the DI and the IVF families was actually generally higher than that in the families with the naturally conceived child. Mothers in the assisted reproductive group were significantly warmer with their children and more emotionally involved and had more positive mother-child interactions. Fathers in that group also had more positive interactions with their child. As Golombok (1999) says, "The findings suggest that genetic ties are less important for family functioning than a strong desire for parenthood. . . . the quality of parenting in families where the mother and father had gone to great lengths to become parents was superior to that shown by mothers and fathers who had achieved parenthood in the usual way" (p. 432).

There is also research comparing parental functioning of lesbian couples who conceived using DI with heterosexual parents who conceived naturally. Flaks, Ficher, Masterpasqua, & Joseph (1995) compared fifteen pairs of each group, whose children were between three and nine years old. The two groups of parents were found to be quite similar in terms of their adjustment as a couple. As for parenting skills, the lesbian mothers showed more awareness of what is required for effective parenting than did the heterosexual parents. (It should be noted, however, that both the lesbian and the heterosexual mothers were superior to the heterosexual fathers in this respect.) There were no deficiencies found in the lesbian mothers, even those who had no biological ties to the child.

A comparison of seventeen lesbian couples and seventeen heterosexual couples with children under the age of two found that the lesbian couples shared parenting responsibilities more equally than did the heterosexual couples (Hand, 1991). The nonbiological lesbian mothers were significantly more involved in childcare than were the (biological) heterosexual fathers. A similar design was used to compare gay male couples who had chosen parenthood with heterosexual couples (McPherson, 1993). McPherson examined twenty-eight gay and twenty-seven heterosexual couples and found that the gay fathers reported sharing parenting tasks more equally than did the heterosexual couples.

Among gay and lesbian parents, the fact that there is at least one parent with no biological tie to the child may actually serve as a motivation for the nonbiological parent to have a high degree of involvement with the child. The nonbiological parent may feel he or she must work harder to establish a tie with the child. The biological parent may be particularly sensitive to his or her partner's position and may endeavor to foster the relationship between the child and the nonbiological parent.

There has been one study that looked at how lesbian mothers explained their children's conception to them (Mitchell, 1998). Of the thirty-four mothers in the sample, two-thirds had conceived their child through DI, while the remainder of the children had been conceived in an earlier heterosexual marriage or had been adopted. When their children were between the ages of three and six, they began asking questions about how they came to be. The DI mothers reported that they explained the process as truthfully and age-appropriately as they could, and most felt comfortable in doing so. While we should be careful not to draw too many conclusions from a single study, it is clear that most children conceived via DI by lesbian mothers will know, from a very early age, that a donor exists somewhere.

In the few studies that have looked at parenting within gay and lesbian families, a clear pattern has emerged: Parenting does not suffer. In fact, in those studies that find a difference, parenting in gay and lesbian families is superior to parenting in families whose children were naturally conceived. Although one partner of any couple that conceives a child through DI will not be biologically related to that child, that partner does love the biological parent. No evidence suggests that a nonbiological parent feels less close to or committed to that child than a parent who is biologically related. For parents who create their families using DI or who adopt their children together, both parents are involved in the process of planning for the child, and both are present as soon as the child enters the family. They undertake the job of parenting together, and they tend to develop their own rules, expectations, and routines together.

What remains a question is how the child will feel as she comes to understand that her biological father exists and that she may never come to know him. This is, of course, similar to the process that adopted children go through.

Adopted Families

There are two reasons to discuss adoption as it relates to gay and lesbian parents. First, many gay men and lesbians choose adoption as the method for creating their families. Findings that apply to adoptive families in general have relevance to them. Second, children in adoptive families deal with many of the same issues—such as having a parent with no biological tie and having an unknown biological parent—that face children in many gay and lesbian families. In fact, at least one expert in the field views DI as "semi-adoption" (Melina, 1989).

Are adoptive parents as close to their children as birth parents? Existing data generally indicates that they are. In a study that compared security of attachment in infancy, adopted infants were found to be as likely to be securely attached to their adoptive mothers as were children who were born to their parents (Singer, Brodzinsky, Ramsay, Steir, & Waters, 1985). A large study, which looked at 881 adolescents, found that adolescents who had been adopted during infancy were doing as well as their nonadopted siblings in psychological adjustment and positive family relationships (Benson, Sharma, & Roehlkepartain, 1994).

However, it has been well documented that adopted children, as a group, show higher rates of emotional difficulties and learning problems than do nonadopted children (see Verhulst & Versluis-Den Bieman, 1995; Wierzbicki, 1993). Several explanations have been offered to account for this. Poor prenatal care and genetic influence have been mentioned as biological triggers of later problem behavior. It has also been suggested that adoptive parents are more likely to seek professional help for their children than are nonadoptive parents. It has even been hypothesized that mental health professionals are likely to perceive adopted children's behavior as more problematic (see Brodzinsky, Smith, and Brodzinsky, 1998, for a discussion).

Psychologists have described a life cycle for adoptive families in general, identifying particular tasks for both adoptive parents and their children at different stages (Brodzinsky, Smith, and Brodzinsky, 1998). Prior to adoption, parents come to terms with their infertility, make the decision to adopt, and begin to explore their own thoughts and feelings about the birth parents. Once the child arrives, the parents take on the identity of mother or father and begin integrating the child into the family. During the preschool years, the parents begin telling the child about her adoption, and the child starts to understand it. In middle childhood, children comprehend the ramifications of having been adopted. They begin to examine their own thoughts and feelings about their birth parents and to recognize that their experience is unusual. Parents' tasks are to foster a positive view of the birth family without undermining the child's connection to her adoptive family. During adolescence, adoptees integrate their adoption into their personal identities, and some consider instigating a search for their birth parents. At this time, parents continue to help their adolescent cope with the fact of her adoption. Some parents focus on helping their child maintain realistic expectations about her birth parents and supporting her plans to contact them. Others counsel against such plans.

While at this point it is speculation, a similar process may be at work in families created through DI. As children's cognitive and social capacities develop, their understanding of what it means to have been conceived by DI, and their feelings about that, will also change. As DI children grow up, they will probably go through a process similar to the one that adopted children go through.

Studies on transracial adoptions show that most adoptees develop a healthy self-concept that includes aspects of both their birth culture and the culture in which they were raised (Simon, Altstein, & Melli, 1994). Many gay men and lesbians create their families through adoption, and many of these adoptions are transracial. Moreover, in a way, gay and lesbian adoptions are similar to transracial adoption. In both cases, the families do not look like typical families. In both cases, at least some family members are part of a minority group to which the children may not belong. And, in both cases, family members may straddle different social and cultural groups. Not a great deal has been written about gay and lesbian adoption (see Ricketts & Achtenberg, 1990, for an exception). Currently, three states (Florida, Mississippi, and Utah) prohibit gay men and lesbians from adopting, while seventeen states allow second-parent adoptions.

While there are many similarities, there are also some important differences between adoptive families and families that were created by DI. In both cases, there is a biological parent who is unknown to the child, and possibly even to the parent or parents. While open adoptions and sperm donors who are willing to be contacted once the child reaches adulthood are becoming more common, some families will always lack information about one or both of a child's biological parents. In the case of adoption, often what is unknown is not only information about the birth parents but also information surrounding the child's birth. Was the pregnancy unplanned; was the baby abandoned; was the mother forced by her own family or culture to give up her baby? Not only is the identity of the parents unknown, but the story of how the child came to be is missing, as well. In contrast, with DI children, only the identity of the father is unknown. The story of how the child came to be is one the child knows very well—his mother or mothers wanted a child very much, they chose a donor, and here he is. It may be that adopted children will ultimately show more curiosity about their birth parents because they have more questions.

We should mention an important caveat in our discussion of adoption and donor insemination. The level of openness can vary considerably within families that were created by these methods. Open adoptions, where the birth mother and sometimes the birth father maintain contact with the child throughout her life, are becoming more common. Sperm banks seem to be going in the direction of giving their clients more information about the donors, in some cases including photographs and audiotaped interviews, as well as a great deal of background information. Some sperm banks are offering the option of allowing children to contact their donors once they reach adulthood. Some lesbian couples choose men they know as donors. The amount of contact these known donors have with the child can range from none to constant, with the donor functioning as a father. The particular level of information about and the amount of contact with her biological parents that a child has will obviously have a great impact on how she deals with the situation. As more lesbians choose to become parents through DI, more children will grow up with the knowledge that they have a biological donor whom they may never know.

Stepfamilies

When heterosexual couples with children divorce, often one or both of the parents remarry. The effects of divorce and parental remarriage on children have been well studied (see e.g., Hetherington & Clingempeel, 1992; Wallerstein & Corbin, 1989; Wallerstein, Lewis, & Blakeslee, 2000). While parental divorce is stressful for all involved, studies have shown that children fare best when the custodial parent maintains an authoritative parenting style and does not expose the child to parental conflict (Buchanan, Maccoby, & Dornbusch, 1991). When heterosexual parents remarry or have a new partner who resides with them, the arrival of a stepparent creates a new family. How well children adjust to this development depends in part on the child's age and gender, support from people outside the family, and the child's own temperament.

Among heterosexual-headed families, the most common type of stepfamily is the biological mother/stepfather family. Boys tend to adjust better to this type of arrangement than do girls (Hetherington, 1993; Hetherington, Cox & Cox, 1985). In terms of children of different ages, those who find adjusting to stepfamilies most difficult are those in early adolescence (Hetherington, 1993). Over time, mother-child relationships in stepfamilies become more harmonious and less conflicted (Hagan, Hollier, O'Connor, & Eisenberg, 1992).

There has been less research on biological father/stepmother families, in part because these families are less common. Children in these families typically have a harder time dealing with their new family constellation. However, children who live with their fathers after a divorce also tend to have more problems to begin with, so it is not clear whether the father/stepmother dynamic itself tends to be more problematic (Brand, Clingempeel, & Bowen-Woodward, 1988).

Much of the research that has been done on children of gay men and children of lesbians has actually been done on children living in gay or lesbian stepfamilies. These children were born into a heterosexual relationship; that relationship ended, and one parent subsequently entered into a gay or lesbian relationship. There are valid reasons for studies to have been conducted this way. Courts have become involved in settling child custody disputes and have needed information on how children fare in such families. Also, until recently, when increasing numbers of gay men and lesbians began creating their families within the context of their gay or lesbian relationships, researchers have had to rely on stepfamilies for their data.

Given what we know about stepfamilies, we could predict that children living in gay or lesbian stepfamilies would be as at least likely to experience problems as children in heterosexual stepfamilies. In fact, it could be argued that perhaps children living in gay or lesbian stepfamilies might be expected to show more problems than children in heterosexual families, since the former have the additional task of dealing with their parent's change in sexual orientation.

Golombok, Spencer, & Rutter (1983) assessed twenty-seven lesbian mothers and twenty-seven divorced heterosexual mothers and their children. They found no differences between the groups of children on measures of emotions, behavior, and relationships, although they did note a slight tendency for the children living with heterosexual mothers to exhibit more psychiatric problems. As in earlier studies, the lesbian mothers were more likely to be living with a partner than were the heterosexual mothers.

Huggins (1989) compared the self-esteem of thirty-six adolescents, half of whom were living with their lesbian mothers and half with their heterosexual mothers. There were no significant differences in self-esteem between the two groups of adolescents. Interestingly, in both groups, those adolescents whose mothers were currently living with a partner showed higher self-esteem than those whose mothers were single. As we have seen before, more of the lesbian mothers were living with new partners than were the heterosexual mothers.

More recent studies have looked at the dynamics involved in lesbian stepfamilies. Wright (1998) gives a detailed account of five lesbian stepfamilies, based on interviews, observations, and family members' journals. She found that the families dealt with issues common to all stepfamilies, such as differences in approaches to discipline, difficulties in dealing with the ex-husband, and difficulties meshing different personalities. The families also dealt with unique issues related to being lesbian families, including creating a role for the stepmother, dividing tasks on some basis other than gender, and living in a broader culture that assumes everyone is heterosexual. The approach of this study marks a significant departure from that of earlier ones in that it focuses on family dynamics.

Summary

Families that were begun by donor insemination or adoption or after a divorce and the beginning of a new adult relationship, all share certain characteristics and challenges. In each of these families, there is at least one parent who has no biological tie to the children. In many of them, one parent has no legal tie to the children. These characteristics do not necessarily lead to problems in the parent-child relationship; indeed, as we have discussed, several studies suggest that a better parent-child relationship exists in these families. It seems clear that the lack of a genetic or biological link between a parent and a child does not, in itself, pose a risk for difficulty.

[3]

Are the Children Normal?

A question that has been asked, in many different ways, about children being raised by gay men or lesbians is, Are they normal? That is, how do these children compare to their peers who have heterosexual parents? Is their experience so far removed from that of children raised by heterosexual parents that they differ in some fundamental ways from those children? Or, are there subtle distinctions between children of gays and children of heterosexual parents, distinctions that may become evident only once the children reach adulthood?

The adjustment of children raised by gays or lesbians is of more than academic interest. Public discourse, legislation regarding adoptions, and decisions made in courtrooms all rest in part on beliefs about how the children in these families fare. We, then, examine the studies that have looked at this question: Are the children normal?

Intellectual Functioning

It is not clear what rationale would be used to suggest that children raised by gay or lesbian parents might be lacking in their academic skills, intelligence or general cognitive functioning, and, indeed, none has been advanced. However, some studies of children of gay and lesbian parents have included measures of intellectual functioning. Flaks, Ficher, Masterpasqua, & Joseph (1995) compared fifteen three- to nine-year-old children born to lesbian couples with fifteen children of the same age born to heterosexual couples. No differences were found on IQ scores between the groups (IQ was assessed either through the Wechsler Intelligence Scale for Children-Revised (WISC-R) or the Wechsler Preschool and Primary Scale of Intelligence, the two most frequently used measures of children's intelligence). Likewise, Green, Mandel, Hotvedt, Gray, & Smith (1986) found no differences on IQ measures between fifty-six children who lived with lesbian mothers and 48 children living with heterosexual mothers, and Kirkpatrick, Smith, & Roy (1981) found no differences in WISC-R IQ scores between children of lesbian mothers and children of heterosexual mothers in their study of twenty children, ages five to twelve, in each group.

Peer Relationships

Concerns that children with gay or lesbian parents will experience difficulties with their peers, which might range from teasing to harassment to outright ostracism, have been cited by some judges who are reluctant to grant custody to a gay or lesbian parent.

Do children of lesbian and gay parents experience hostility from peers during their early years? When the children in their sample were school age (between five and seventeen years), Golombok, Spencer, & Rutter (1983) collected information about their relationships with other children. (This sample contained thirty-seven children of lesbians and thirty-eight children of heterosexual mothers.) The two groups of children did not differ in the quality of their peer relationships, according to interviews with their mothers. Only two in each group were described as having definite problems with other children. About one-third of the children were described as having some slight difficulties with peers, which included things like being shy or getting into more than the usual number of quarrels.

Green, Mandel, Hotvedt, Gray, & Smith (1986) asked both mothers and their children about their social relationships. Children of lesbian mothers were as likely to rate themselves as popular as were children of heterosexual mothers. The ratings of the lesbian and the heterosexual mothers did not differ, either; they were equally likely to rate their children as sociable and accepted by other children.

These studies were conducted on school-age children. Other studies have focused on adolescence, a period in which developing positive relationships with peers and coping with the need to belong are critically important developmental tasks. Adolescence is thought to be the period when, if ever peer difficulties are going to occur, they will occur. Adolescents are coming to terms with their own sexuality and are thought to be especially sensitive to issues related to sexuality (Deevey, 1989).

Tasker & Golombok (1997) interviewed the young adults in their sample about their experiences with peers during adolescence. Teasing was a common experience for both groups: more than three-quarters of adolescents in both groups reported having been teased. They found that those with lesbian mothers were no more likely to recall having experienced teasing than were those with heterosexual mothers. Of those in both groups who were teased, there was no difference between the groups in whether they categorized the teasing as serious and prolonged. For young women, there were no differences between the lesbian mother group and the heterosexual mother group in whether they had been teased about their mother's sexuality or about their own. The sons of lesbian mothers were more likely to have been teased about their own sexuality than were the sons of heterosexual mothers. It may be that any association with homosexuality has more negative implications for boys than for girls. For adolescent males, there is a great deal of pressure to be seen as virile and heterosexual. Having a lesbian mother appears to cause other adolescents to question a young man's own sexuality, or at least pretend to question it.

Psychological Health

The argument that children raised by gay or lesbian parents are likely to develop interpersonal or emotional difficulties is based on two assumptions. The first is that children in these families will experience teasing and ridicule from their peers, which will lead to social isolation and disturbed peer relationships. The second assumption is that the experience of having gay or lesbian parents is in itself so stressful that it will lead to anxiety, depression, or other types of psychological maladjustment.

Researchers have looked at the psychological adjustment of children in gay- and lesbian-headed homes. No differences between children ages three to nine raised in two-parent lesbian homes and children raised in two-parent heterosexual parent homes were found on measures of behavioral adjustment (Flaks, Ficher, Masterpasqua, & Joseph, 1995). The children's behavioral adjustment was assessed by each child's biological mother and by each child's teacher, each of whom completed questionnaires that asked about three areas of the child's behavior: internalizing behavior (which includes problems such as depression, anxiety, and fearfulness); externalizing behavior (which includes problems such as aggression, disobedience, and hyperactivity); and social competence (which includes positive behavior such as getting along with peers). In no case was there any significant difference between children of lesbian parents and children of heterosexual parents.

Golombok, Spencer, and Rutter (1983) assessed two groups of children via extensive psychiatric interviews of the children and their mothers. Both groups of children (with rare exception) had been born into a heterosexual relationship and later been through a parental divorce. The mothers of one group of children were now living as lesbians, while the mothers of the other group were living as single heterosexual parents. All of the children now resided with their mothers. The mean age of the children was nine and ten years. No differences between the groups were found in the children's emotional development, behavior, or relationships as assessed by mother or teacher questionnaires. In no case did the children of lesbians fare worse than their counterparts. In facts, according to the maternal interviews, the children of single heterosexual mothers were more likely to have been referred to a psychiatric clinic (although it must be noted that only a small number of them had been referred). Once again, the children in the "lesbian mother group" were living with a parent in a relationship, while the children in the "single heterosexual mother group" were not. This methodological confound is one that appears frequently in studies on lesbian mothers and their children. We discuss the implications of this more fully in chapter 5.

A similar study, which examined children living with lesbian and with heterosexual mothers, was undertaken by Kirkpatrick, Smith, and Roy (1981). The children were between the ages of five and twelve, most had been through a parental divorce, and they and their mothers were assessed by a psychologist. The children were also assessed by a psychiatrist. No differences were found between the two groups of children in terms of emotional disturbance or presence of pathology.

Adolescent children of lesbians have also been studied in terms of their psychological health. Gershon, Tschann, and Jemerin (1999) measured the self-esteem of adolescents who were living with their lesbian mothers. Most of the adolescents had been born into heterosexual marriages. Their parents' marriages ended, and their mothers assumed lesbian identities. The results showed that this group's self-esteem scores, including their feelings about their own self-worth, close friendships, and social acceptance, were within the normal range.

Similar findings were reported by Huggins (1989), who found no difference in self-esteem between adolescents with divorced heterosexual mothers and adolescents with divorced lesbian mothers.

Researchers have also examined the possibility that children raised in lesbian or gay households might not exhibit psychological adjustment difficulties until later in life. That is, even if no psychological maladjustment is apparent during childhood, some problems may appear during adulthood. Tasker and Golombok (1997) examined this question and found no differences in either anxiety or depression (measured by the Trait Anxiety Inventory and the Beck Depression Inventory, respectively) between the two groups of young adults they assessed (one group had been raised by lesbian mothers, the other by divorced heterosexual mothers). The young adults raised by lesbian mothers were no more likely to have sought professional mental health treatment. Gottman (1990) found that adult daughters of lesbians scored within the normal range on measures of social adjustment and did not differ from women who had been raised by either single or remarried divorced mothers.

To summarize, in no study that has looked at the psychological well-being of children raised by lesbian mothers has there been any evidence to suggest that the children are maladjusted. Overall, studies that have assessed children, adolescents, and young adults have found that this group is functioning well. While this answers the question "Are the children normal?," the topic of psychological health can be examined in a more subtle and nuanced way.

Looking at whether one group differs from another in some way is what psychologists call looking at between-group differences. Comparing the psychological adjustment of children raised by lesbian mothers to that of children raised by heterosexual mothers is an example of research that studies between-group differences. Another type of research looks at variation within a particular group. This type of research, which looks at individual differences within a particular group, is also being conducted with children of lesbian mothers. This latter type of research goes beyond looking at whether the children appear normal and begins to look at what other factors are associated with good adjustment among these children.

Correlates of Psychological Adjustment among Children of Lesbian Mothers

Patterson (1995a) looked at twenty-six families of lesbian couples with children. These children, who had a mean age of six, had been born or adopted into their families. Patterson found that children's adjustment was related to how their mothers divided childcare activities. When both the biological and the nonbiological mothers shared childcare responsibilities evenly, the children fared best. Mothers were also more satisfied when the role sharing was more egalitarian. Chan, Brooks, Raboy, & Patterson (1998) found that it was the parents' satisfaction with their division of labor, rather than the actual division of labor itself, that was associated with children's adjustment. Specifically, in their sample of thirty lesbian couples with children, the nonbiological mother's satisfaction was related to lower rates of children's behavior problems.

Huggins (1989) found that adolescents of both lesbian and heterosexual mothers reported higher self-esteem if their mothers were currently living with a romantic partner. Her findings also suggest that the father's attitude toward the mother's lesbianism plays a role in the adolescent's self-esteem. The age at which the adolescent learned of her mother's lesbianism was another factor that affected self-esteem. Generally, daughters who learned that their mothers were lesbian during early childhood had higher self-esteem than did those daughters who found out in later childhood or early adolescence.

Gender in the Gay and Lesbian Family

One area that elicits a great deal of concern in terms of gay and lesbian parents is that of gender. A particular concern is the impact on children of growing up without role models of one particular gender; of being denied the opportunity to bond with a parent of the same sex (or the opposite sex, as the case may be); or of being unable to learn how boys and girls are "supposed to" act. Gender development is very complex and has biological, psychological, and social components; these include gender identity, or one's concept of oneself as male or female; gender-role behaviors, or activities that differentiate between males and females; and sexual orientation, which has been defined as a primarily heterosexual, homosexual, or bisexual orientation. It is a field of study that has undergone considerable transformation in the past twenty years.

The three components of gender have not always been viewed as separate, and even psychologists have sometimes used different terms interchangeably. While in some cases there is overlap, the three dimensions of gender development are quite separate. Someone with problems with gender identity may wish or believe that he or she would be happier as a member of the opposite sex. Someone who enjoys participating in activities that are not traditionally enjoyed by members of that person's gender (for example, a male who likes to sew or a woman who enjoys car racing) is said to be engaging in atypical gender-role behaviors. A person's sexual orientation relates to which sex an individual finds emotionally, romantically, and physically attractive.

Even the way psychologists view these entities has changed in recent years. The person most responsible for that change is Sandra Bem, who pioneered work on gender roles and androgyny (Bem, 1974, 1977). Androgyny is the presence of both masculine and feminine traits in the same person. Androgynous people have been found to score better on a variety of psychological adjustment measures (Bem, 1977; Boldizar, 1991). Most androgynous individuals are females, and it seems that women with traditionally feminine traits fare the worst on measures of self-esteem and adaptability (Taylor & Hall, 1982).

The concept of androgyny is an interesting one to consider in terms of gay and lesbian parents. Gay and lesbian parents are obviously not leading traditionally masculine or feminine lives. Gay and lesbian parents cannot divide up chores and activities on the basis of gender, since they share one gender. Therefore, children are by definition exposed to androgynous role models. In addition, gay and lesbian parents may be more likely to encourage androgyny in their children, since they are not living according to traditional gender roles themselves. Stereotypes that suggest that lesbians are masculine in their demeanor and that gay men are effeminate have led some people to hypothesize that children raised by gay or lesbian parents might be likely to have atypical gender role development.

Gender Role

In children, the acquisition of gender roles involves their choices in play and preferences in activities. Traditionally, there are activities that girls prefer, such as playing with dolls, jumping rope, and engaging in imaginative play that involves tea parties and playing house, and activities that boys prefer including playing with cars and trucks and engaging in imaginative play such as cops and robbers or war. Gender-neutral activities include playing with puzzles and collecting objects like seashells or marbles. Hoeffer (1981) looked at the play preferences and activity interests of forty children, half of whom lived with heterosexual single mothers and half of whom resided with lesbian mothers. The average age of the children was eight years, and all had been living without their fathers since before they were five. Children were asked with what toys they preferred to play and what activities they preferred to do. There were no differences between the types of responses given by the children of lesbian and those of the children of heterosexual mothers. Both boys and girls preferred traditionally gender-appropriate toys, and boys were less likely to be interested in playing with gender-neutral toys. Interestingly, lesbian mothers were more willing to encourage their children to play with an equal number of both feminine and masculine toys.

A similar design was used in another study that addressed gender development by assessing forty children between the ages of five and twelve (Kirkpatrick, Smith, & Roy, 1981). Again, half the children were living with single heterosexual mothers, and half were living with lesbian mothers. No differences were found between the two groups of children in history of play preferences or in blind clinical evaluations of problems of gender identity.

Green (1978) examined gender-role identity in a group of thirty-seven children ages three to twenty years. Twenty-one of the children had lesbian mothers, and the remaining sixteen were being raised by a transsexual parent. Thirty-six of the thirty-seven children expressed gender-appropriate preferences for toys, games, and clothing.

No signs of inappropriate gender identity were found in another group of children being raised by lesbian mothers (Golombok, Spencer, and Rutter, 1983). The sample included thirty-seven children in lesbian households and thirty-eight children in heterosexual single-mother households. The gender-role behaviors of boys and girls were quite different from each other and in keeping with expected patterns.

Moreover, similar findings were also reported by Green, Mandel, Hotvedt, Gray, & Smith (1986), who compared fifty-six children of lesbian mothers with forty-eight children of heterosexual mothers. None of the children of lesbian mothers showed any indication of problems in the area of gender identity. Interestingly, while daughters in both groups fell within the normal range in terms of gender-role behaviors, the daughters of lesbians were less traditionally feminine in their choice of clothing and activity preferences. No differences were found for sons. It may be that lesbian mothers encouraged their children in seeking androgynous dress and activities, particularly with their daughters. Girls have more freedom in this area in that they can engage in traditionally masculine pursuits without encountering disapproval. Boys, on the other hand, still face negative responses from others if they are seen to be interested in traditionally feminine activities. It is not surprising, therefore, that girls would show greater flexibility in their choices.

Lesbian and heterosexual mothers have been found not to differ in their descriptions of ideal behavior for children in terms of gender roles (Kweskin & Cook, 1982). No differences emerged in the way mothers described the "ideal" boy or the "ideal" girl, either. In one of the few studies that includes a comparison between lesbian mothers and gay fathers, Harris & Turner (1986) found that gay fathers were more likely to encourage their children to play with gender-specific toys than were lesbian mothers. Again, this suggests that lesbian mothers in particular may be interested in promoting androgyny.

The studies discussed so far have focused on children who, for the most part, were born into heterosexual marriages and whose mothers later took on lesbian identities. It could be argued that these children are not the ideal ones to study if one wishes to assess whether being raised by a lesbian mother puts a child at risk for atypical gender development, since they had spent some portion of their lives in heterosexual families and therefore had been exposed to masculine role models. A better population to sample would be children who have lived their entire lives in lesbian-headed families.

The researcher who has done the greatest amount of work on children of the lesbian baby boom is Charlotte Patterson. She has published extensively on lesbian mothers and their children and is the leading authority on gay and lesbian parenting. Among her studies is one of thirty-seven children born to lesbian couples (Patterson, 1994). Here, too, the children, who ranged in age from four to nine years, all scored within the normal range on gender-role identity.

We have not reported on any studies of children of gay fathers for a simple reason: There aren't any. To date, no one has examined gender-role variables in children in gay-father families. This area is in particular need of research, not only to make up for the general lack of studies on gay men and their children. We speculate that gay fathers may feel more pressure than lesbian mothers to adhere to rigid gender-role expectations for their children. In an essay published in the *New York Times* on March 11, 2001, the columnist and gay father Dan Savage writes of his desire for his son to show interest in the types of masculine toys that he, himself, never did and of his discomfort when anyone suggests that he and his partner are trying to steer their son toward homosexuality. It may be that lesbian mothers are less susceptible to this pressure. Comparisons between gay fathers and lesbian mothers in this area would be most welcome.

Are children of gay and lesbian parents more likely than children of heterosexual parents to grow up to be gay themselves? This question has been asked by many people who oppose gay parenthood. Putting aside for the moment the issue of why this would be a bad thing if it were true, let's examine the question. It could be argued that, if genetics has anything to do with homosexuality, then biological children of gay and lesbian parents might be assumed to be more likely to have the same genetic predisposition for homosexuality that their parents do. In fact, there is some evidence to suggest a heritable component to sexual orientation, particularly in males (see Bailey & Pillard, 1991; Zuger, 1989).

It could also be argued that children of gay and lesbian parents, who grow up with models of adult same-sex relationships, are more open to the idea of such relationships. It could be that children of heterosexuals rarely allow themselves to entertain the possibility of entering a same-sex relationship, while children of gays and lesbians are less inhibited in that way and are more knowledgeable about the reality of these relationships, rather than stereotypes.

Sexual orientation of offspring of gay and lesbian parents has been studied by a number of researchers over the years, and scientists have not found any sign that such children are more likely to be gay or lesbian than are children of heterosexual parents. Adolescents and adult children of both gay men and lesbians have been studied, with similar results. For example, Green (1978), in his study of thirty-seven children raised by homosexual or transsexual parents, inquired about the sexual orientation of the thirteen children old enough to have romantic desires. All were heterosexually oriented. Miller (1979) interviewed a group of gay fathers and found that one son among twenty-one was gay and three daughters of twenty-seven were lesbian. These numbers are not disproportionate to what would be expected in any sample of this size. Huggins (1989) interviewed thirty-six adolescents, half of whom were living with lesbian mothers and half of whom were living with heterosexual mothers. Of the thirty-sex, only one, the child of a heterosexual, identified as homosexual. Bozett (1981) interviewed gay fathers about their children's sexual orientation and found that none of the twenty-five children in question were gay or lesbian.

Gottman (1990) studied three groups of women: thirty-five adult daughters of lesbians who had been raised with a lesbian coparent; thirty-five adult daughters of heterosexual divorced women who had remarried or who had lived with men while their daughters were growing up; and thirty-five adult daughters of divorced heterosexual women who had remained single. The three groups did not differ in the proportions of respondents who claimed homosexual orientations. In all three groups, approximately three-quarters of the women were heterosexual, according to their scores on a measure of sexual orientation.

Bailey, Bobrow, Wolfe, & Mikach (1995) looked at the sexual orientation of adult sons of gay fathers. These researchers suggest that, in order to answer the question of the transmission of sexual orientation, four groups must be studied: sons of gay men, daughters of gay men, sons of lesbians, and daughters of lesbians. They believe that children of different genders may be affected differently depending on whether their fathers or their mothers are homosexual. In their examination of eighty-two sons of fifty-five gay fathers, they found that more than 90 percent of the sons were heterosexual. They also found that the length of the time the sons had lived with their fathers had no effect on whether the sons grew up to identify as gay or straight.

In their study comparing the children of lesbians with the children of heterosexual women, Golombok, Spencer, & Rutter (1983) found that, among the twenty children old enough to express sexual interest, the two groups did not differ on sexual orientation. This same group of children was studied when they were young adults (Tasker & Golombok, 1997). At the time of the follow-up, all of the children with heterosexual mothers identified as heterosexual themselves, and all but two of the young women with lesbian mothers also identified as heterosexual. In their detailed interviews with the young adults, the investigators did find some differences between the groups. In general, those with heterosexual mothers had never considered any alternatives to heterosexuality. In contrast, the young adults with lesbian mothers had given some thought to their mothers' homosexuality and its implications for their own sexuality. They had considered the possibility that they might one day experience an attraction for someone of the same gender or even have a same-sex relationship.

This study suggests that children of lesbians are more open-minded about their own options in terms of their own sexual orientation, but the overwhelming majority still identify themselves as heterosexual as adults.

Summary

No studies suggest that children of lesbian mothers differ from other children in their gender-role development. No studies suggest that a disproportionate number of the children of lesbian or gay parents identify as homosexual in adulthood. In sum, there is no evidence to support the notion that having a gay or lesbian parent places a child at risk for atypical gender or sexual development in any way.

[4]

Family Life in Gay and Lesbian Families

Referring to a group of families, such as gay- and lesbian-headed families, as if they were a homogenous collection of families is misleading. Gay and lesbian families are a diverse group, not only in terms of the usual factors that differ among families, such as economic and racial backgrounds, religious affiliation, and residential area, but also in ways that do not even apply to families headed by heterosexual parents. Gay and lesbian stepfamilies have not only gone through a parental divorce; they have also gone through the process of having a parent come out. Both parents and children must grapple with the issue of whether and to whom they will disclose the parents' sexual orientation. Homophobia has far-reaching effects on these families; it affects child custody decisions and children's participation in activities such as the Boy Scouts or religious groups and can subject families to discrimination on an individual level. Primary gay or lesbian families, or those that were begun in the context of the gay or lesbian relationship, must deal with the ramifications of having a DI or adopted child. While she was writing only about lesbian mothers, DiLapi (1989) could just as easily have been referring to gay fathers as well when she discusses the motherhood hierarchy, which puts the most appropriate mothers (i.e., married heterosexual mothers) at the top and the least appropriate mothers (i.e., lesbian or nontraditional mothers) at the bottom. Many people do not feel that gay men or lesbians make acceptable parents, and this ideology affects those parents and their children.

Not only do gay and lesbian families deal with a unique set of issues; they are in some ways families unlike other families. Two-parent families where both parents are the same gender are not necessarily going to manage the workload along traditional gender lines, as do most heterosexual couples (Cowan & Cowan, 1992). Gay and lesbian parents may be more sensitive to issues of discrimination and intolerance than other parents, and this may affect their parenting. Those individuals or couples who became parents after coming out may have had to face obstacles in adoption or in gaining access to alternative reproduction techniques. They may have faced opposition to their plans, even from their own families and friends. What impact these factors have upon them and upon how they parent their children is an open question. Some gay and lesbian parents are prohibited from having any legal tie to their children; not all states allow two people of the same gender to legally adopt a child together. Whether this leads to the nonlegal parent's feeling less secure in his or her status as a parent is not known. In sum, there are many reasons to examine the inner workings of life in the gay and lesbian family.

Lesbian Stepfamilies

Some of the earliest studies done on children of lesbians compared family functioning in different types of divorced families. Children whose parents have divorced have gone through a number of upheavals in their lives. They have experienced parental discord prior to the divorce; they have lost the presence of one parent in their homes and in their daily lives; generally they have experienced a drop in family income. Lesbian mothers who had children while in heterosexual relationships face different challenges than do divorced women who are heterosexual. The unique circumstances faced by lesbian mothers have been examined by psychologists. The earliest studies tended to focus on how lesbian mothers managed their lives and on how strongly they feared they would lose their children in a custody battle.

Pagelow (1980) studied two groups of mothers who were raising their children following a heterosexual divorce or breakup: those who still identified themselves as heterosexual and those who identified as lesbian. She asked twenty lesbian mothers and twenty-three heterosexual mothers about their experiences regarding child custody, housing, and employment. The lesbian mothers reported more fear about losing their jobs if their sexual orientation were to be discovered and more fears about losing custody of their children. More of the lesbian mothers were living with a romantic partner than were the heterosexual mothers. This raises issues about the different experiences of these families. It may be that a greater percentage of lesbian mothers ended their marriages because of their sexual orientation and with the intention of beginning a new relationship with a specific person. The new lesbian partner, in many cases, may have been present as soon as the divorce proceedings began. Thus, in these cases not only does the newly divorced woman have a new partner to provide support; she is also embracing a new and more satisfying identity. A newly divorced heterosexual woman, on the other hand, has experienced the end of her marriage, and, if she is living without a new partner, as most are, she is without an intimate support. We would expect these different circumstances to have an impact upon the family dynamics; we must keep these differences in mind when looking at studies that focus on divorced women and their children.

Lyons (1983) found, in her study of forty-three lesbian and thirty-seven heterosexual divorced mothers, that lesbian mothers were significantly more fearful of losing custody of their children. A similar result was found by Lewin (1984), who interviewed forty-three lesbian and thirty-seven heterosexual divorced mothers. The mothers did not differ on variables such as relations with extended family or ex-husbands or in their feelings about their status as divorced mothers.

While parents' fear of losing custody of their children because of their sexual orientation has not entirely disappeared since these studies were completed, it is safe to say that the fear is less widespread. According to the National Center for Lesbian Rights, a parent's sexual orientation is no longer reason enough for custody to be denied. Still, the possibility that an individual judge in a particular case may allow homophobic notions to sway a decision on child custody still elicits concern.

Moving beyond a focus on worries about custody and living arrangements, other researchers have looked at factors associated with good functioning in lesbian mothers. Rand, Graham, & Rawlings (1982) examined the psychological health and well-being of twenty-five lesbian mothers. Greater psychological health was significantly related to greater openness about their sexual orientation with their children, ex-husbands, employers, and the lesbian community. The happiest lesbian mothers, then, were those who were the most open and most accepting of themselves. The authors did not specify how many of these mothers were cohabitating with a partner.

Miller, Jacobsen, & Bigner (1981) compared responses of thirty-four custodial lesbian mothers to those of forty-seven heterosexual mothers when presented with hypothetical caregiving situations. They found that lesbian mothers were more child oriented in their approach to dealing with children. The authors speculate that because lesbian mothers fear the social stigma their children will experience, they are more nurturing and concerned with their children's feelings.

Lott-Whitehead & Tully (1992) assessed family functioning in forty-five lesbian mothers' families. Half of the mothers had conceived their children within a heterosexual relationship. When asked about their concerns regarding their family, very few (only three) mentioned fear of losing custody of their children because they were lesbian. The most common response in terms of being a lesbian family was concern over how the world will treat the child. The strengths of their families included an open climate for sexuality and a respect and tolerance for differences, including but not limited to sexual orientation. Most of the mothers scored in the moderately high to very high range on a measure of family stress. However, many of these were single mothers, so there may well be other factors that contributed to the relatively high stress levels.

Primary Lesbian Families

Family functioning within primary lesbian families, which we define as families that were begun within the context of a lesbian relationship, has been assessed by a number of researchers. These families have not gone through a divorce or the formation of a new family, and so studies focusing on them do not have to worry about the confounding effects of those variables. Studies that focus on families that have never included fathers provide important information about lesbian motherhood. The parents in these families have not gone through the emotional turmoil that lesbian stepfamilies have and so offer a "purer" look at lesbian family life.

An interesting study was undertaken by Golombok, Tasker, & Murray (1997), who compared lesbian mother families, single heterosexual mother families, and two-parent heterosexual families. Their interest was to assess family functioning in fatherlessness families. They found that the mothers in the fatherless families showed greater warmth with their children, and interacted more with them, than did the mothers in the two-parent heterosexual families. The children without fathers were also more likely to be securely attached to their mothers. There were no differences among the three groups of children in terms of emotional or behavioral problems or peer acceptance. The researchers did not rely solely on reports of parents but also included direct assessments of the children and reports from their teachers.

The children from fatherless families indicated that they felt less competent cognitively and physically than did the children of heterosexual parents. The authors suggest that fathers may be more likely than mothers to praise their children's academic and physical accomplishments; on the other hand, children in fatherless homes may perceive their families as being less valued by society than families that have a father present. It could be that this perceived lack of approval from others manifests itself in feelings of decreased competency in those areas. Taken together, the study results suggest that being raised without a father poses no ill effects for mother-child relationship or children's psychological health, though the children may exhibit slightly lower self-esteem in certain areas.

Researchers have been interested in looking at how parents in two-parent families where both partners are female handle the workload that comes with having children. Patterson (1995a) looked at parents' division of labor in her study of twenty-six lesbian families, all of which had at least one child between four and nine years old. She found that the lesbian mothers in her sample generally divided up tasks in a fairly egalitarian way. The more evenly the parents shared the childcare tasks, the more well adjusted the children were. At the same time, the biological mothers reported more involvement with childcare, while the nonbiological mothers spent more time at their jobs. Even with this tendency, however, Patterson reports that household and child-rearing responsibilities are shared more evenly in lesbian couples than in heterosexual couples.

Patterson and her colleagues (Chan, Brooks, Raboy, & Patterson, 1998) continued looking at parental division of labor, parental satisfaction, and children's psychological adjustment among lesbian couples, but they added a creative twist. For a control group, they used heterosexual couples who had also conceived their child using an anonymous donor. In their study, then, they had in each family a biological mother and a parent who was not biologically related to the child. They found that the lesbian parents divided childcare responsibilities more evenly than did the heterosexual parents, even though all parents worked a similar number of hours in paid employment. In this study, the nonbiological lesbian mothers did not spend more time in paid employment than did the biological lesbian mothers. This finding contradicts Patterson's (1995a) results. What this suggests is that, among lesbian couples where both partners spend an equivalent amount of time in the workforce, the partners tend to share work inside the home evenly, as well.

Stiglitz (1990), in a small study that involved seven lesbian couples and five heterosexual couples, looked at the impact of the birth of a first child upon the adult relationship. She found that parents in both groups expressed dissatisfaction with the loss of freedom and time alone. She also found that heterosexual mothers felt satisfied with the support they got from their own families and with their connectedness with the community, while lesbian mothers reported that they felt more like a separate family. These findings are based on a very small number of subjects, but they do suggest that there may be differences in lesbian mothers' experience of social support.

Gartrell and her colleagues (Gartrell, Hamilton, Banks, Mosbacher, Reed, Sparks, & Bishop, 1996; Gartrell, Banks, Hamilton, Reed, Bishop, & Rodas, 1999; Gartrell, Banks, Reed, Hamilton, Rodas, & Deck, 2000) have undertaken a longitudinal study of lesbian families whose children were conceived by DI. This study, begun when the prospective mothers were pregnant or undertaking the process of insemination, has the potential to yield valuable information about the developmental course of lesbian family life. The 1996 study found that couples had been together an average of six years prior to attempting pregnancy. The initial sample included 154 prospective mothers: seventy two-mother families and fourteen single-mother families. Prior to the child's birth, 78 percent of the participants anticipated that at least some members of their own family would accept the child; 15 percent expected that no relative would accept the child. More than half the participants intended to be completely open about their lesbianism when raising their children, and the remainder planned on being relatively open. They cited concerns about raising a child in a lesbian family, given that the child would be living in a homophobic and heterosexist society, and about the effect on the child being raised in a nontraditional family.

When the children were two years old, a follow-up study (Gartrell, Banks, Hamilton, Reed, Bishop, & Rodas, 1999) found that the majority of the mothers were out to the children's pediatricians and caregivers. Three-quarters of the two-mother families reported sharing childcare responsibilities evenly. Nearly half the mothers felt that two-mother families were more likely to have two highly involved parents than were two-parent heterosexual families. Nearly 90 percent of mothers planned to enroll their children in educational programs that included children and teachers of diverse racial, cultural, and economic backgrounds. They felt that exposing their children to diversity was the best way to inoculate them against homophobia.

The study did highlight some areas of concern. More than half of the mothers worried about how their children would deal with the fact that they were conceived by DI. Sixty-four percent reported feelings of jealousy and competitiveness about bonding with the baby. As this is a longitudinal study, future reports will show how the mothers handle these issues. Many cited disappointment with the lesbian community's acceptance of their families; only 58 percent felt that their families were welcomed by their local lesbian community. This suggests that lesbian mothers are at risk for a lack of social support, even within their own families and communities. How they manage this-whether they establish other supportive relationships to compensate for the nonsupportive ones, try to change the attitudes of nonaccepting others, or simply go without that needed acceptance-remains to be seen.

By the time the children were five years old (Gartrell, Banks, Reed, Hamilton, Rodas, & Deck, 2000), 31 percent of the original couples had broken up. As a point of comparison, among children of heterosexuals, about 50 percent are expected to be living with a single parent at some point in their lives, and nearly one-third of marriages end within ten years (Chadwick & Heaton, 1999). Thus, this sample's rate of marital dissolution is comparable to what would be expected of a heterosexual sample.

Of those couples who were still together, 68 percent reported that the child was equally close to both parents. Parents reported sharing childcare equally in most cases, and nearly all felt that their partners had similar philosophies regarding child rearing. The majority (87 percent) of the children were said to be getting along well with their peers. Nearly one-fifth (18 percent) had already experienced some homophobia from either peers or teachers. Sixty-three percent of the children had grandparents who openly acknowledged their lesbian family, while in a minority of cases (17 percent of birthmothers and 13 percent of nonbiological mothers), the grandparents did not fully accept the grandchild as a member of the family.

Gay Fathers

Fewer studies have been conducted on families headed by gay fathers, but there have been some. The earliest studies tended to focus on dispelling homophobic myths about gay men as parents. Miller (1979), in his study of forty gay fathers, for example, concluded that gay men do not sexually abuse their children; they do not have children in the first place to camouflage their homosexuality; and they do not "contaminate" their children by leading them into a homosexual life. The issue of disclosure of gay fathers' sexuality to their children was also a topic of great concern in the early literature. Bozett (1980) interviewed eighteen gay fathers, all of whom had had their children within heterosexual relationships. Not all of the fathers had disclosed their homosexuality to their children.

The ones who had not disclosed cited fear of rejection by their children; their own lack of acceptance of their sexuality; and a fear of vindictiveness on the part of their ex-wives. The fathers who had disclosed their homosexuality to their children cited their desire to foster a close, intimate relationship with their children, part of which meant being open about themselves.

In a comparison between thirty-three gay fathers and thirty-three heterosexual fathers, Bigner & Jacobsen (1989) found few differences in the fathers' parenting behaviors. They did find that gay fathers were generally more strict with and at the same time more responsive to their children. Gay fathers were more willing to extend themselves to promote their children's participation in social activities. Heterosexual fathers were more willing to be demonstrative with their current partner than were gay fathers. The same researchers (Bigner & Jacobson, 1992) in a different study, found that parenting styles and attitudes toward fathering did not differ between twenty-four gay and twenty-nine nongay fathers.

Comparisons between Gay and Lesbian Parents

As we have seen, a popular approach in much of the research we have discussed so far has been to compare a group of gay or lesbian parents to a group of heterosexual parents (for example, divorced lesbian mothers and divorced heterosexual mothers). The implicit assumption in this type of design is that the heterosexual group of parents represents the normal or control group, and then the gay or lesbian group can be measured against them. This is a useful approach in that it can provide evidence that children do not suffer harm when they have gay or lesbian parents. However, such studies do not give us information about how gay fathers and lesbian mothers compare with each other. A handful of studies have examined similarities and differences between gay fathers and lesbian mothers.

Harris & Turner (1986) is one such study, although its participants were very few; the researchers compared ten gay fathers, thirteen lesbian mothers, two heterosexual fathers, and fourteen heterosexual mothers. An interesting twist to their study was that they distributed questionnaires in such a way that respondents could remain anonymous if they chose to do so. Gay fathers reported greater satisfaction with their first child and fewer disagreements with their partners over disciplining their children than did lesbian mothers. Lesbian mothers felt, more than gay fathers, that their children would benefit from growing up with homosexual parents. Specifically, they felt that their children would be more empathic and tolerant toward others, more open to different points of view, and more accepting of their own sexuality. In another study, Turner, Scadden, & Harris (1990) conducted structured interviews with ten single gay fathers and eleven single lesbian mothers. Lesbian mothers were found to earn significantly less money than gay fathers. They were also more likely to have disclosed their homosexuality to their children.

Summary

The study of family life within gay and lesbian families initially focused on issues of disclosure and child custody. Recent studies suggest that parents' fear of losing custody of their children because of their sexuality has diminished but not entirely disappeared. Most of the studies done so far have concluded that there are few differences between homosexual and heterosexual parents. What differences have emerged, however, suggest that gay and lesbian parents tend to be more responsive to their children, more child oriented, and more egalitarian in their sharing of the workload, characteristics associated with a more positive child outcome.

[5]

The Challenges of Studying Gay and Lesbian Parents

A number of issues face psychologists as they embark upon research. They must investigate their area of interest; design their study, deciding which measures to use; locate a group of participants willing to be in the study; and analyze and interpret their findings. Psychologists who wish to study gay and lesbian parents and their children must do all of these things, but, in addition, they face certain challenges because of whom they are studying. In some ways, gay and lesbian parents and their children are more difficult to study than are other families.

Finding Study Participants

Psychologists who conduct research all face the challenge of finding people who are willing to be participants in their studies. In ideal circumstances, psychologists are able to locate a sample, or group of participants, that is representative of the population, the larger group they are interested in studying. For example, a researcher who is interested in studying how toddlers learn language obviously cannot assess all toddlers' linguistic abilities. He or she must find a group of toddlers who are typical of children that age and whose parents are willing to let them participate in the study. The researcher would like to find a diverse group of toddlers-not all children from wealthy families in cities, and not all children of impoverished single parents, but a cross-section of children from different familial, social, racial, and economic backgrounds. Ideally, the researcher could look to census data to determine whether the sample is representative in terms of demographic variables such as family income, parents' marital status, and so on.

Psychologists interested in studying gay and lesbian parents and their children have the same ultimate goal: to study a group of participants who resemble the larger group of all gay- and lesbian-headed families. The first difficulty arises because no one knows what the larger group of gay and lesbian parents looks like. Are most of these parents living in what we call gay or lesbian stepfamilies, as has long been the assumption among researchers? Patterson (1995c), for example, states: "Probably the largest group of children with lesbian and gay parents today are those who were born in the context of heterosexual relationships between the biological parents, and whose parent or parents subsequently identifies as gay or lesbian." (p. 265). Are there more lesbian mothers than gay fathers? By what method do most lesbians and gay men choose to become parents? There is no definitive answer to these questions, because there has been nothing comparable to a large national study, like a census, to answer them.

Researchers must therefore be mindful of the lack of data on the population of gay and lesbian parents as they draw their conclusions.

For example, as we have noted, most studies done on gay and lesbian parents and their children have been done on stepfamilies. The findings of these studies certainly apply to the population of gay and lesbian stepfamilies, but it is not certain whether they also apply to primary gay and lesbian families. Stepfamilies have gone through two major upheavals-divorce and the addition of a new stepparent-that intact primary gay and lesbian families have not. Researchers who have worked with these stepfamily samples are always quick to point out the limitations of their samples, and readers of these studies must keep them in mind.

Locating a sample of gay and lesbian families is also a bit more involved than locating, say, a sample of families with toddlers. Researchers typically use some standard methods to recruit participants for studies. Depending upon the type of respondents they wish to include, these may include advertising in community newspapers; posting flyers where they will likely be seen by the target group (for example, putting flyers on the bulletin boards of preschools if the researchers wants to study three-year-olds); or attending meetings where the target group is likely to gather, such as PTA meetings or support groups relevant to the researcher's interest. If the target group is gay and lesbian parents or their children, the best place for a researcher to start is with support groups for those families. Many researchers contact local parenting groups in order to find participants for their studies. This certainly makes a great deal of sense: If you want to study gay and lesbian parents, go where gay and lesbian parents are. However, we must not lose sight of the issue of representativeness. What proportion of gay and lesbian parents are involved with support groups? Are those who are involved different in some ways from those who are not involved? It may be that parents who are involved in such groups tend to be the ones who are the most open about their sexual orientation and the proudest of their families. On the other hand, it could be that parents who are having the most difficulty dealing with the ramifications of being gay or lesbian are the ones who are looking to parenting groups for support. If the first hypothesis is true, this could mean that studies that focus on families who are involved in support groups could paint a rosier picture than is actually true. On the other hand, if the second hypothesis is true, then gay and lesbian families are functioning better than the studies would indicate. It could also be the case that the support groups for gay and lesbian parents contain a mixture of both well-functioning and troubled parents, and therefore the difference washes out.

There are certainly gay and lesbian parents who would never dream of joining a group, either because they are living in areas where there are few, if any, other gay or lesbian parents or because they do not choose to be publicly identified as gay or lesbian. There is very little information on gay and lesbian parents who are in the closet, simply because they are in the closet. Some researchers have attempted to devise ways of maximizing their chances of locating such people. Harris & Turner (1986), for instance, devised a system of using color-coded questionnaires for homosexual and heterosexual parents. All participants were encouraged to take questionnaires of both colors in case they knew someone who might be interested in completing them. It was the researchers' hope that this would enable gay or lesbian parents who did not wish to be publicly identified as such to participate in the study. But, generally speaking, the difficulties associated with contacting gay and lesbian parents who have not come out about their sexual orientation have meant that few such parents have been included in research.

This is important, because closeted gay and lesbian parents may be more at risk for feelings of isolation and a lack of social support. Their children may feel that they must keep their parents' sexual orientation a secret, and they may be less likely to be open about and proud of their families. Until more studies are done that make it possible for gay and lesbian parents outside the network of parenting groups to participate, these will remain matters of speculation.

Number of Participants

A related issue that has plagued much of the research on gay- and lesbian-headed families is that of small sample size. Generally, the largest sample size in the research we have discussed has been in the area of forty parents. Some studies have been published with as few as five participants. Studies done with a relatively small number of participants are not necessarily a problem. As Patterson (1995b) has pointed out, what is important is the pattern of results that many studies have found. No studies to date have found children of gay or lesbian parents to be functioning less well than children of heterosexuals. However, studies with more participants have more statistical power, which means they are more likely to be able to find differences if they are there. Put simply, having more study participants means one can have more confidence in one's results.

Cohort Effect

In developmental psychology, there is a phenomenon known as the cohort effect. This refers to the fact that people of different ages have different life experiences. What may look like the effect of maturation may, in fact, have nothing to do with maturation and everything to do with the different times in which they grew up. For example, imagine that a researcher was interested in studying political attitudes of people at different stages of life. Suppose she questioned a group of seventy-year-olds and a group of twenty-year-olds and found that the younger people were more liberal in their attitudes. Would she be justified in concluding that people become more politically conservative as they get older? She would not, and the reason is that the seventy-year-olds in her sample had life experiences completely different from those of the twenty-year-olds. It could be that the seventy-year-olds were just as conservative when they were in their twenties as they are now, or even more conservative. This is an example of the cohort effect. The time at which people were different ages has a profound effect upon them.

In terms of studying gay and lesbian parents, we must be aware of the cohort effect. Studies that were done on children of gay men and lesbians in the 1970s and 1980s may have limited relevance for children who are growing up now with gay and lesbian parents. Conditions have significantly changed over the past thirty years. Thirty years ago, there were very few gay and lesbian parents living openly and few if any support groups and almost no legal protections available to them. Currently, there are many more openly gay and lesbian parents, there are national organizations, as well as local groups, dedicated to support and advocacy on their behalf, and there is increased acceptance of homosexuality in general. We can expect children of today to be doing even better than the children of years ago. Psychologists may wish to explore issues that were investigated in the past, in order to see how much things have changed for gay- and lesbian-headed families. When examining results of studies done in the past, it is important to keep in mind when the studies were done. We believe, that studies done in the 1980s, for example, that found that children of gay and lesbian parents were functioning as well as children of heterosexual parents suggest that today's children are probably functioning at least that well now, and possibly better.

Cross-Sectional and Longitudinal Studies

Psychologists can use two basic research designs: cross-sectional research or longitudinal research. In cross-sectional studies, the most common type of design, participants take part in the study once, and then they are finished. This design allows the researcher to get information about the people in the study at a particular point in time. In longitudinal studies, participants agree to take part in the study at different points across time. They may, for example, complete a set of questionnaires every year for five years. This enables the researcher to follow one group of people, examining how they change and develop over the course of the period of study.

Both designs have their advantages and their disadvantages. Cross-sectional studies are relatively quick to do and allow for comparisons between different groups of people (for example, a study may include three-year-olds and six-year-olds). A limitation of cross-sectional research is that it offers a snapshot of the participants at a single point but does not show their progression. Longitudinal research is all about progression. It follows a group of people over time and allows the researcher to determine what factors at an earlier time caused other factors at a later time.

It was not until recently that longitudinal studies of gay and lesbian families were undertaken. No one study can answer all the questions there are about gay and lesbian families. Each one has its own strengths and weaknesses. What is important is the pattern of results that these studies show, and the addition of longitudinal research can only serve to strengthen that pattern.

Control Groups

When looking at a sample that is thought to be unique in some way, researchers would like to have a group with which they can compare that sample. Ideally, researchers would like to have two groups that are similar in every way except the one under study. Then, the researcher can conclude that any differences that emerge between the groups must be the result of the one way in which the groups differ. The second group, which is used as a comparison, is known as a control group. It may seem obvious to us that a good control group to use when studying gay- and lesbian-headed families is families with heterosexual parents, but the issue is a bit more complicated than that. Researchers who study lesbian stepfamilies often use single-mother divorced families for comparison. This is not ideal, because lesbian mothers are more likely to have new partners than are heterosexual mothers. In this case, the two groups differ not only in terms of the mothers' sexual orientation but also on the presence of a stepparent. Differences between the groups may be due to either of those factors.

Some researchers have shown very creative and thoughtful approaches to the problem of finding truly comparable control groups. Chan, Brooks, Raboy, & Patterson (1998) and Golombok, Cook, Bish, & Murray (1995) have used heterosexual parents who conceived their children via anonymous DI as a control group for primary lesbian mothers. The goal of these researchers was to find a group that truly was similar to the lesbian mothers in all ways, including the method of conception, except for the sexual orientation of the parents. These researchers accept the importance of using an appropriate control group and have found a way to achieve it.

Summary

There are challenges that are unique to studying gay and lesbian parents and their children. No study is perfect, and no study can hope to be immune to criticisms of one kind or another. There are obstacles to overcome in studying gay and lesbian families, but these obstacles can be and have been dealt with by creative and sensitive researchers. As we review them, we should keep each study's limitations in mind and focus on the unique contribution each study makes to our understanding of gay and lesbian parents and their children.

[6]

The National Study of Gay and Lesbian Parents

W e set out to do a study that would tell us about family life for gay and lesbian parents in the United States today. We were interested in hearing about how these parents came to form their families, what difficulties they had experienced or expected to experience, what strengths they saw in their own families, and what their priorities were as parents. Very few studies have examined these issues among gay- and lesbian-headed families, and none had done so with a large national sample.

We recruited participants in three ways: through advertisements placed in national magazines; through contact with local gay and lesbian parents' support groups around the country; and through postings on Internet sites of interest to gay and lesbian parents. We were hopeful that using the Internet to attract participants would allow gay and lesbian parents living in relatively isolated areas to participate in our study. In order to be eligible to participate in the study, participants were required to identify themselves as gay or lesbian and to be the parent of at least one child under eighteen who lived with them. Those who were willing to participate and who fit the study criteria were mailed questionnaire packets. We assured our participants that only those of us working on the project would have access to their addresses and that we would destroy the addresses once we mailed the packets to them. We took this step to ensure total confidentiality for our respondents. Completed packets were returned in postmarked envelopes.

Method

Demographic Information

Participants completed a two-page questionnaire that asked for basic demographic information, including gender, educational background, and occupational status, as well as family background. The questionnaire was designed specifically for this study.

Relationship Measures

Respondents who were in a relationship completed a survey called the Dyadic Adjustment Scale (Spanier, 1976). This scale is a widely used assessment of the quality of couples' relationships. The thirty-two-item scale includes four subscales: consensus, which refers to the level of agreement on issues of importance to the couple; satisfaction, which refers to their level of satisfaction with the relationship; cohesion, which refers to how united each member of the couple feels with the other;

and affectional expression, which refers to overt physical affection between partners. The survey also has an overall scale of global satisfaction, which is the sum of the four subscales.

Coupled respondents also completed a two-item assessment of the division of child-rearing and housekeeping tasks, based on the measure used by Hetherington and Clingempeel (1992). Each participant indicated how much responsibility he or she had in terms of the daily tasks of caring for the children and of maintaining a household. Responses were given on a seven-point scale, with a score of "1" meaning the subject does it all, "4" meaning the subject and his or her partner share equally, and "7" meaning the subject's partner does it all.

Parenting Measures

The Parenting Alliance (Abindin & Brunner, 1995) is a twenty-item questionnaire that assesses the degree to which the respondent feels united with his or her partner when it comes to dealing with their child(ren). We used this in conjunction with the Gay Parenting Assessment, a measure designed for this study that asks open-ended questions about the subjects' experiences as a gay or lesbian parent. The assessment covered topics including the reactions of family and friends to their parenthood, their openness with others about their sexuality, and their own concerns about raising a child in a gay or lesbian home, as well as their beliefs about the benefits to their children of having a gay or lesbian parent. We encouraged our participants to write as much as they felt necessary to answer the questions completely. We also used the Parenting Practices Survey (Holden & Zambarano, 1992), which assesses the parents' use of specific disciplinary techniques during a typical week. This is answered on a seven-point scale (0 = never to 6 = nine or more times).

Together, these questionnaires enabled us to develop a detailed picture of family life within gay and lesbian families. It was our goal to reach a broad sample of these parents, and not merely to confine our respondents to those who were living in a few gay-friendly enclaves. We chose some questionnaires that have been widely used before, to enable us to compare our respondents' answers to established norms. We also created our own questionnaires to ask specifically about issues relevant to gay and lesbian parents and to allow them to describe their own perceptions.

The Sample of Gay and Lesbian Parents

The final sample consisted of 415 participants: 79 males and 336 females. This group represented 256 families. For the men, there were twenty-five two-parent families where both parents participated, twelve two-parent families where one parent participated, and seventeen single-parent families. For the women, there were 134 two-parent families where both parents participated, thirty-eight two-parent families where one parent participated, and thirty single-parent families.

The participants came from thirty-four states (California, Texas, Pennsylvania, New Jersey, Arizona, Iowa, Ohio, Kansas, Virginia, Massachusetts, Illinois, New York, Florida, South Carolina, Georgia, Vermont, Minnesota,

Wisconsin, Tennessee, New Mexico, Oregon, Washington, Arkansas, Maryland, Colorado, Missouri, North Carolina, Louisiana, New Hampshire, Alabama, Connecticut, Indiana, Wyoming, and Hawaii), as well as the District of Columbia. The men ranged in age from twenty-five to fifty-two, with a mean age of forty-one. The women's ages ranged from twenty-two to sixty-five, with a mean age of thirty-eight.

The overwhelming majority of subjects were white (94 percent). Four percent identified themselves as Hispanic. Those identifying themselves as African American, Native American, or other numbered at less than 2 percent. Thirty-eight percent of the sample described the area where they

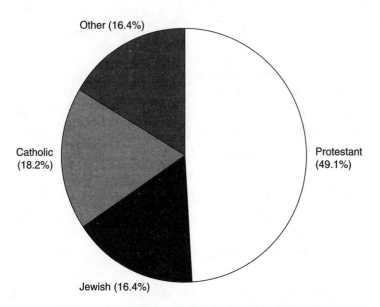

FIGURE 6.1. Religious Affiliation of Male Subjects

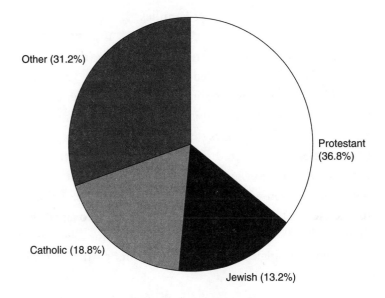

FIGURE 6.2. Religious Affiliation of Female Subjects

live as urban, 48 percent as suburban, and 14 percent as rural. Twenty-eight percent of the sample identify themselves as Protestants, 13 percent as Catholics, 10 percent as Jewish, and 20 percent as having another religious affiliation (most commonly Unitarian); and 30 percent reported having no religious affiliation (see Figs. 6.1 and 6.2).

This sample was well educated. Among the men, 12 percent had some college, 37 percent were college graduates, and 49 percent had obtained a graduate degree. Among the women, 18 percent had some college, 30 percent were college graduates, and 48 percent had earned graduate degrees (see Figs. 6.3 and 6.4).

Types of Families

Of the 256 families represented in the sample, the majority (146, or 57 percent) had been formed within the gay or lesbian relationship. This proportion did not vary significantly between the gay and the lesbian parents (see Tables 6.1 and 6.2). We found that families that had begun within gay or lesbian relationships differed significantly from those begun in heterosexual relationships in some basic ways. Not surprisingly, the children who had been born into heterosexual families tended to be older than the children born into gay or lesbian families. The adult relationships (that is, the relationship between the biological parent and his or her partner) were of

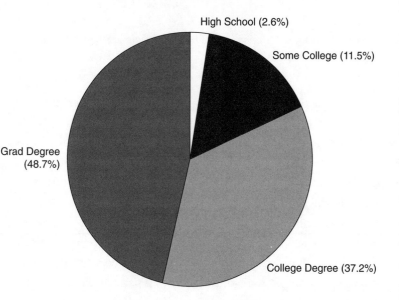

FIGURE 6.3. Education Level of Male Subjects

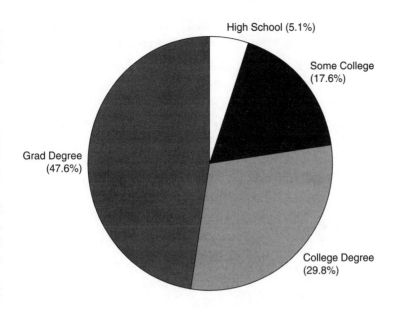

High School (5.1%)

Some College (17.6%)

Grad Degree (47.6%)

College Degree (29.8%)

Figure 6.4. Education Level of Female Subjects

shorter duration in the families where the children had been born into a heterosexual relationship. In a very real way, this sample consisted of two groups of gay and lesbian parents: those who had borne their children in heterosexual relationships, whose children were now in late childhood, and who (if they were not single) were in a relatively new same-sex adult relationship; and those who were in well-established same-sex adult relationships (if they were not single), who had had children in that relationship, and whose children are currently just entering elementary school. Since these different types of families have different backgrounds and children of significantly different ages, we discuss their experiences separately where appropriate. For simplicity, we refer to those families that began within the context of a gay or lesbian relationship as "primary gay" or "primary lesbian" families. The families that began within the context of a heterosexual relationship are called "gay stepfamilies" or "lesbian stepfamilies." Those few families that do not fit into either category (almost in-

TABLE 6.1

Type of Family: Male-Headed Families

	Number	Percentage
Primary gay	30	56
Gay stepfamilies	18	33
Blended (children from both heterosexual relationship and gay relationship)	0	0
Other	6	11

TABLE 6.2

Type of Family: Female-Headed Families

	Number	Percentage
Primary lesbian	115	57
Lesbian stepfamilies	59	29
Blended (children from both heterosexual relationship and lesbian relationship)	16	8
Other	12	6

TABLE 6.3

Family Demographics by Type of Family

	Length of Adult Relationship (average no. of years)	Age of Oldest Child (average no. of years)
WOMEN		
Primary lesbian	9.7	4.8
Lesbian stepfamilies	3.4	11.5
Blended (children from both heterosexual relationship and lesbian relationship)	7.8	14.1
MEN		
Primary gay	13.0	5.9
Gay stepfamilies	4.2	15.6

variably individuals who became parents while they were single) are referred to as "other" (see Table 6.3).

In the following chapters, we present both statistical analyses of our data and verbatim transcriptions of our participants' written responses describing their experiences. In some cases, minor editing for clarity has been done, but otherwise all quotations are exact. We feel that gay fathers and lesbian mothers are the ones best suited to talk about their families, and we are happy to allow them to do so.

[7]

Creating a Family

We were eager to explore how gay and lesbian parents came to become parents in the first place-not only how it came about, but what their decision-making process had been, what options they had considered, and what kind of responses to their plans they had received from others. Whether as a gay or lesbian couple choosing to have its own child, a single adult deciding to adopt a child, or a divorced parent electing to enter into a gay or lesbian relationship, these parents did not create their families in the usual way. We asked them to tell us how they did it.

Coming Out First, Having Children Second: Families Begun in a Gay or Lesbian Relationship

Frequently, lesbian mothers and gay fathers said that their desire to have children was something they discussed from very early on in their relationship with their partners. On average, the lesbian mothers had been together for five years before they had or adopted a child. The gay fathers had been together, on average, even longer before starting their family: seven years. They had often discussed the possibility for many years before actually beginning the process.

We talked about it from the start of our relationship. My partner had always wanted kids; I needed to be persuaded. We decided after I had gotten tenure that we would actually begin the process seriously (about eight years into the relationship).

I have always wanted to raise children, as has my partner. We talked about it on our first date.

We began discussing having children shortly after we met seven years ago, and we began actively seeking sperm donors about two years ago.

I knew I wanted to have children long before our relationship. It took some convincing of my partner, since she had never considered it an option before. It was a joint decision when we started the process one year into our relationship.

I had initially wanted children but then decided against it for fear of not being fair to the child being raised in a lesbian household. My partner always wanted children. We went through two years of therapy together to try to resolve the issue. No resolution was really reached except I more or less resigned myself to the fact that she was going to try regardless. She tried three times with my help and was unsuccessful. At the doctor's office it was successful, resulting in one miscarriage and one pregnancy. Our daughter was born in 1998, and we're both very happy.

It is clear that the decision to become parents was not made lightly by these parents. A great deal of thought and discussion had been undertaken prior to their making the final decision. Participants often spoke about their concerns, even prior to having children, about the impact of having gay or lesbian parents on their children. Many cited a lifelong desire to become parents and a long wait until they were fully prepared to begin the process. In some cases, one partner was more invested in becoming a parent than the other. In such cases, it took some time for the second partner to make the commitment to parenthood, as well.

After deciding to become parents, the next step was deciding how to become parents. For gay or lesbian couples who have made the decision to become parents, the issue of how they will accomplish their goal is a complex one. Those who wish to become biological parents must determine (in the case of two women) which one of them will become pregnant; whether they will use a known or an unknown sperm donor; and, if they use a known donor, how much contact he will have with the child. For men, the issue of which one will be the biological father is coupled with the task of locating a woman willing to be a surrogate and navigating the legalities surrounding that arrangement.

The other possibility for gay men and lesbians is to become parents through adoption. This method has difficulties of its own. Many adoption agencies refuse to work with gay or lesbian couples. Foreign adoption, in general, is not something that gay men or lesbians can pursue openly as a couple-generally, one member of the couple presents him- or herself as a single person who wishes to adopt. In many cases, the agency in this country that assists with the adoption is aware of the situation but deliberately does not make the foreign country aware of it, as this would immediately disqualify the applicant. All adoptions require that the prospective parent submit to a home study, where a social worker visits the home and interviews the applicant in order to determine whether he or she would be a fit parent.

In most states, only one parent in a gay- or lesbian-headed household can be the legal parent. This leaves one parent without legal rights or status regarding the child, whether the child is the biological offspring of one parent or has been legally adopted by one of them. This has the potential to create an imbalance between the partners, as the one without legal ties may feel excluded from the parent-child relationship.

Among the primary gay and lesbian families in our sample, the men and the women chose different paths to parenthood. Most of the mothers in our sample chose to become pregnant using an anonymous donor. Eighty-eight percent of the primary lesbian mother families conceived their own children. Many mentioned their strong desire to give birth to their own children as the reason for choosing this option.

I felt strongly about having a child. I couldn't wait to be pregnant.

I always wanted to experience pregnancy but would have had a child in any way.

I always wanted to give birth.

Some also mentioned their concerns that adopting a child might be impossible, or very difficult, for them as lesbians. Many of these women felt that adoption was not a real option for them because they would not be considered suitable applicants. Others felt strongly about not wishing to submit to the scrutiny of outsiders evaluating their fitness as prospective parents.

Adoption seemed out of the question for two lesbians. Besides, I wanted the experience of having my own child.

I was clear that I wanted to have a child, and felt reluctant to deal with home studies and the expense of adoption. We considered a known donor but weren't able to work that out.

When we started thinking about it, we were open to all options. We went for the biological, as we originally thought it would be the least complex and intrusive from a legal and social perspective.

I never cared how a child would enter my life-biologically or through adoption-it never mattered. I always wanted to parent and knew I would. My clock had run out when we were finally ready, and biology was more cost-effective than adoption, so we chose a donor (from a bank) and inseminated at home.

I never believed I'd have a child whatsoever, since knowing I was lesbian at twenty. However, the lesbian baby boom became common, and I suddenly had a choice. I was clear I would try for pregnancy first, rather than submit to someone else's approval in the adoption process.

The decision as to which woman will bear the child was an easy one for most lesbian couples to make. We had anticipated that this decision might be an emotionally challenging one for many couples, but this did not turn out to be the case. Only 4 percent of the lesbian mothers reported any difficulties in deciding who would actually have the child. The most commonly given reason was desire. In nearly half the cases (46 percent), one woman wanted to become pregnant and the other did not.

We had no difficulty deciding she would conceive, as she had always wanted to and it had never crossed my mind.

It worked well because I always wanted to carry and my partner never really cared if she did or not.

In almost a third of the lesbian couples who used DI to start their families, one partner's age or health was the determining factor in deciding who would have the child.

My partner is more than ten years older than me, and I was the one who wanted children. She supported me 110 percent. I was in my early thirties when we began discussing children. She always felt she was too old.

The women in my family tend to have difficult pregnancies. My partner and I decided she was the ideal one to have them. We wanted full siblings, so she had both.

It was relatively easy to decide, as my partner knew she had infertility issues (discovered in a heterosexual relationship). I offered that she try first and receive medical treatment, but she chose not to-too emotionally difficult.

Absolutely not. She (1) was postmenopausal, (2) has had spinal surgery, and (3) is too butch!

In one family, concern about how the child would be treated by extended family members played a role in the decision about which partner would bear the child.

Initially my partner thought she wanted to carry the child. We both quickly and easily decided I would carry. My parents had no grandchild and would accept the child easier if I carried it.

In some families, both women wanted to bear a child. Possibly they both felt a strong need to experience pregnancy or to have a child with a biological link. Some mentioned the desire to create a family balanced in terms of the parental bond. We suspect that our prediction, which was that deciding which partner would bear the child would be a difficult one for many couples, did not turn out to be on target because, in those couples where both had a strong desire for biological parenthood, the solution was that both would bear a child.

My partner was eager to carry the first child. I gained courage and peace by watching her and carried the second. Each of us carrying a child gives an added dimension to our relationship and parenting.

We had to discuss it, of course. My partner's urgency and desire was somewhat greater than mine, but as I'm older, and had less assurance of family support for any child not biologically mine, we decided I should go first, then she would try.

She is a few years older, so we decided to have her go first. I was a little jealous at the beginning because I've always wanted to be pregnant.

Lesbian couples have an obvious advantage in childbearing in that (barring advanced age or medical problems), both partners generally believe that either of them could become pregnant. When that turns out not to be the case, the flexibility of having another potential mother as a partner can pay off.

Early on, we didn't know how to manage it, but we both wanted to conceive and carry a child to birth. My partner is older, so she tried first. She was unable to conceive, however. After several years of trying, we came to a time where I felt ready to try and she was willing to let her need go.

For the first child, she was very supportive of me getting pregnant. After numerous failed attempts of me getting pregnant a second time, and a failed adoption attempt, she offered to try and get pregnant. She admitted to wanting to have the experience! Initially, I was very threatened by giving up what I considered by be my role.

I tried first because I am four and a half years older (my clock was expiring!). I had child #1 at thirty-six. Then my partner tried to get pregnant, and we realized she needed the help of a specialist, i.e., time and money, so I tried again. I had child #2 at thirty-eight.

Adoptive Mothers

Among the lesbian mothers, about half of those who chose adoption did so as a first choice in creating a family. Some mentioned a strong wish to care for a child that needed a family and an unwillingness to bear a child.

Adoption was always our choice. The only issue was whether foreign or domestic, and if domestic through DSS [Department of Social Services]-foster care or arranged private adoption.

Adoption-I *never* wanted to be pregnant.

I considered trying to get pregnant but decided to adopt to give a child that was already in this world a good home. Age was another factor-I think I am too old at forty-two.

I was never interested in being a biological mom and always thought there were plenty of kids who needed homes.

Others came to choose adoption after attempts at conceiving a child failed.

My partner was more interested in being pregnant and having a biological link to the baby. She also thought it would help her family feel like it was their grandchild. But we also knew fertility would be hard because my partner had breast cancer and chemotherapy at thirty. She tried to conceive, and had four years of infertility. Then I tried and got a huge ovarian cyst. Then we met our first daughter's birthmother, who was looking for adoptive parents for her unborn baby.

We tried to have a biological child but couldn't. When we were offered an adoptive placement, we said yes immediately.

We tried to have our own at first, but it just didn't take. Then the opportunity to adopt came up, and we started our paperwork. We were able to have our daughter when she was two hours old.

I myself always wanted to adopt. My partner and I were unsure if we would be able to in our state and tried artificial insemination at first, then adopted.

Our research suggests that once a lesbian couple decides to become parents, the way they accomplish that goal is almost a foregone conclusion: In most cases only one partner is willing or able to carry a child. When both partners wish to carry a child, again the solution is obvious: Both partners attempt to achieve a pregnancy. It was very rare for these women to have any disagreements between themselves as to who would bear the child. When both wished to have a biological child, the only decision seemed to be who would go first. Lesbian women who become parents through adoption do so for the same reasons that heterosexual people choose to adopt: Either their own efforts at conceiving have been unsuccessful, or they wish to give a child who is already in the world a loving, happy home.

Gay Fathers' Choices

A greater percentage of gay fathers than lesbian mothers picked adoption as their method of choice for creating a family. More than 85 percent of the families of gay fathers were formed through adoption. Obviously, it is more difficult for a gay male to have a biological child than for a lesbian to have one. Finding a woman who is willing to be a surrogate mother is much more difficult than finding a sperm donor. The risks of surrogacy are great; some states do not recognize contracts between prospective parents and surrogates, and the media abound in stories like the Mary Beth Whitehead case, where a surrogate mother reneged on her agreement and sought custody of the child. There is the option of coparenting, where a gay men acts as a donor for a woman (in some cases a lesbian and her partner), with the expectation that he will share in the parenting of the child. This situation entails its own legal risks, in that one party may wish to have more or less involvement with the child than initially agreed upon. Another possible downside to this type of arrangement is that the father will not be a full-time custodial parent. Awareness of the potential difficulties associated with the use of surrogate mothers may lead some gay men never to seriously consider biological parenthood.

We decided to adopt six months into our relationship. The impetus was witnessing the baptism of a six-month old Guatemalan boy, adopted by a (then) single gay man. We always wanted a foreign adoption.

I never wanted "my own." There are too many children that need love.

We always wanted to adopt internationally. We did not want an open adoption or a biological child.

We thought our only option was to adopt. Other options were very expensive.

We wanted to adopt an older child, but no agencies would work with us. Instead, we were chosen by two separate bio-mothers.

Even though it can be very difficult for gay men to become biological fathers, many of the men who ultimately adopted did consider becoming birth fathers.

I wanted to adopt; my partner was interested in coparenting. We chose to adopt so that we both would have an "equal" relationship to our kids.

Adoption was always the main option for us, though we did briefly consider coparenting with a woman friend and having a child biologically (one of us, at least), and decided against it.

We originally thought surrogacy would be our only option (as two gay men) but discovered a private adoption agency willing to work with us. It helped that this agency has one of the best reputations in our state. Through our networking with that agency, a young woman approached us about being a surrogate. Not knowing if the agency process would work (it was an open adoption agency where the birth parents pick the adoptive parents), we decided to pursue both opportunities. Both worked, and we have two children.

First we attempted to use a surrogate mother, but she never became pregnant. Then we got licensed as a foster care family and adopted a foster child.

A small number (six) of gay fathers in our sample did achieve parenthood through the use of surrogacy or through a coparenting arrangement with a woman.

We wanted to have our own child through surrogacy. That was always our first choice. Adoption was a secondary option, and one we never had to explore. We thought I would be the sperm donor while we networked for an egg donor and gestational surrogate. But when my sister said she would be the egg donor, naturally my partner became the sperm donor. We were, and are, delighted about that choice (our number one preferred way of doing it.)

I was willing to do it any way possible, although biological fathering became an option and has points to recommend it. My daughter's mother was a single, straight female friend who also wanted a child and was getting older and singler.

In 1990 we started planning on having a child with a lesbian couple-friends of ours. We are godfathers to one of the woman's two kids.

We started talking about adoption. Expense and "home study" issue led to surrogacy option.

Gay Men and Surrogacy

In our sample, there were only a few fathers who had become parents through surrogacy-having a woman bear their own biological child (six families had at least one of their children through this means.) None of the two-parent families indicated that there had been any difficulty in deciding which partner would be the biological father

We both tested OK (viable sperm) but neither of us had a strong preference. We considered mixing but decided paternal certainty might help with the legal issues. In the end, my partner "fathered" the child because he had better health insurance at the time.

We both thought I should be the birth father.

It was pretty much decided in the beginning that I would try first for some time with the surrogate. After the first child my partner would decide if he wanted to have a child biologically. We're exploring that possibility right now.

My partner wanted to father the child. I was fine with that.

For most of the gay men in our sample, however, the costs of becoming biological fathers were too high. The path most of them took to parenthood was adoption. The group of primary gay fathers (those who began their family after coming out) thus differed in several ways from the group of primary lesbian mothers. Gay fathers more often had to go through an adoption agency or facilitator and allow their fitness as parents to be evaluated, and they were more likely to become parents of a child from a different racial background or of an older child. Lesbian mothers did not find the costs of biological parenthood as prohibitive. They were much more likely to give birth to their own children. For them, the "unknown" variable as to their children's biological parentage was the father, as most of the lesbian mothers chose an anonymous donor.

Concerns of family members of fathers who used surrogacy generally centered around the risks of using a surrogate. Surrogacy is a relatively new phenomenon, and the reality is that there are dangers associated with it. The possibility that the surrogate might renege on the original agreement must be considered. The legality of surrogacy varies from state to state. Some family members also wonder (as do prospective parents) how the surrogate mother will be integrated into the family and the child's life.

Just the usual concerns about surrogates changing their mind, spread by the media through Mary Beth Whitehead–type stories.

They were concerned that the surrogate would run off with the baby and I would never see them again. There were a variety of doomsday predictions.

Most of these fathers did not experience anything more than temporary anxiety from their family members, followed by acceptance.

The experience was just as we anticipated. My mom was concerned, mostly about social issues of two men with a baby. My dad was fairly quiet about it, but I'm sure he felt the same way. But they have come around and love the baby. My partner's parents were very supportive from the start (so much so that his father donated thousands of dollars to the surrogacy process).

My mother did ask, "Aren't you concerned that he may turn out to be gay because his biological mother is a lesbian and you're gay?" And, without skipping a beat, my partner responded, "As far as we know, it takes two straight people to have a gay child." That quieted her.

The experience of becoming surrogate fathers, in terms of the medical process and dealing with hospital staff, went smoothly for most of these families.

All the doctors and support people were very supportive and friendly. We were practically celebrities in the nursery at the hospital and given extra-good treatment by the nurses.

The physician who did the insemination was gay himself and had adopted a child.

Occasionally, some problems did arise.

Two physicians had problems with the surrogacy arrangement. One felt it was unethical to provide prenatal care and charge the surrogate's health insurance knowing she would surrender the baby. The other physician (ironically a lesbian and parent herself) was uncomfortable performing the insemination. I suspect she viewed surrogacy as a form of exploitation of women.

As more gay men become parents through surrogacy arrangements, medical professionals have begun to be more accepting. Not all doctors or infertility specialists are comfortable dealing with this situation, but prospective parents who are tenacious appear to be able to locate specialists who will assist them in their effort to become parents.

Family Reactions

We asked the subjects about the type of responses they anticipated and received from others regarding their plans to raise
children. For this set of analyses, only responses from those
parents who had begun their families within a gay or lesbian
relationship were considered. (Obviously, those who had become parents while in a heterosexual relationship did not face
the same type of scrutiny regarding their desire to have a family as did those who were already living in a gay or lesbian relationship.)

Anticipation: What Will My Family Think?

As can be seen in Table 7.1, women were more likely to anticipate negative reactions from their families regarding their
plans to have a child. More than half the women expected to
face some opposition to their plans from their own family
members. Often the concerns or criticisms were couched in religious or politically conservative terms.

Both our families are relatively conservative-they all were not
happy about our commitment celebration (except my gay
brother). I anticipated there would be difficulties with understanding our motivation to have kids, and some fear that we would.

My parents are big Southern Baptists in Mobile, Alabama-not a
gay mecca. Somehow my parents have never accepted gays. Their
position is "Let the gays serve in the military, so the good folks
don't die." We have the "don't ask, don't tell me about your life"
policy.

TABLE 7.1

Responses from Others: Parents in Primary Gay or
Lesbian Families

	Mothers	Fathers
ANTICIPATE NEGATIVE REACTIONS		
From own family	101 (54%)	15 (34%)
From friends	33 (18%)	8 (18%)
From employer	49 (27%)	3 (7%)
EXPERIENCE NEGATIVE REACTIONS		
From own family	81 (44%)	12 (27%)
From friends	44 (24%)	10 (23%)
From employer	17 (9%)	2 (5%)

To my parents I am an unmarried mother. My family has a sort of "don't ask, don't tell" policy. I knew they would be very tearful and worry that I wasn't going to heaven.

I was afraid they'd not be supportive because of the "differentness" of the situation. I was also initially afraid that they would treat the child differently than the rest of the children in the extended family.

With our oldest, it wasn't as common as it has become. We knew we were breaking new ground, so to speak. We also knew that family members whose religious beliefs weren't inclusive would not understand.

I am not in contact with my family as I have chosen to "divorce" myself from them. However, I strongly believe that they would react negatively to the idea of gay parenting. In the past, family members have expressed homophobic comments, which leads me to believe that they would not accept the idea.

I knew it would be an education for them, and I'd have to be very sure about it. But mostly it was all so new to them, and me too in some ways. Mostly they were worried for us. We dreaded talking to them and practiced it over and over.

I'd mentioned the idea to my parents before I even met my partner, and they'd made it clear that they didn't think it would be "fair to the children." They also indicated that they felt I'd given the matter insufficient thought-that it was a whim I'd regret when the responsibility became a burden.

My gay brother believes we should do everything straight people don't, and he doesn't like children. He thought we were just acting straight ("breeders").

Family members often raised concerns about a child's being raised by two women and how it might cause difficulties down the road. They feared that the child would be stigmatized, teased, or ostracized. Given that gay men and lesbians are still the targets of prejudice, this is certainly not an unfounded fear. Perhaps because of advances in civil and legal protection for gays and lesbians in recent years, there has also been vocal opposition to gay rights. Some states and localities (Colorado, for example) have passed or attempted to pass legislation repealing gay rights. Incidents like the murder of Matthew Shepard, a gay young man who was tortured and killed by two homophobic young men in Wyoming, have also drawn attention to the animosity that some people feel toward gays and lesbians. It is no wonder that some family members fear exposing children to these prejudices.

My mom was very surprised and a little negative and still is a little. She said she is worried about how the child will have to deal with a lot of people making fun because her parents are gay.

They all asked if we had really considered what he would have to face when he was older-if we really thought about it.

My mom wanted to know how we were going to safeguard my partner's [the nonbiological mother's] interest. She also asked questions about "What if it's a boy?" and "How will the children deal with it?"

My father said to my mother, "Why do they want to do this? Do they just want to have a gay child?" To which my mother responded, "We weren't gay, were we?"

They were happy to have grandchildren. They might have had some concerns about how the children would be responded to and treated by others.

In some cases, the mechanics of donor insemination, along with the legal hurdles, were cited as concerns by family members. While women who use an anonymous donor are given information about him, in some cases the information is minimal. And, in the end, an anonymous donor is anonymous. Prospective mothers are planning on becoming pregnant by a man they don't know and will often never meet, and this bothers some family members. In addition, they may have concerns about the risks the woman is taking (although the donor is tested for sexually transmitted diseases, including AIDS, concerns still exist on the part of some people).

Dad was concerned about using an anonymous donor until the baby was born. He had unspoken concerns over using switched samples at the clinic. He was concerned we didn't know who we were using.

My parents were freaked out that I had insemination with anonymous donor sperm.

Some of the women chose not to discuss their plans to have a child prior to conception. For women who were undergoing artificial insemination, waiting until they were pregnant, or even later, to tell their families was not uncommon. In most cases, they expected opposition from their families and wished to avoid having to listen to arguments trying to dissuade them from the decision.

My sister knew of my plan to conceive. I didn't tell anyone else about attempting artificial insemination until afterwards. I told everyone in the family when I was three months pregnant. I never discussed my plan with anyone but my sister. I did not want to experience any reactions. I felt it was my decision.

I thought my mother would try to declare me unfit. I told my mother when my child was three months old.

We expected both of our parents to be negative. Mine were involved almost from the beginning, and came to accept. My partner's weren't told until I was three months pregnant.

I didn't tell them until I was five months pregnant. I couldn't handle the stress. I wrote them a letter. They called about five days after getting the letter. I'm sure they were crushed. They are very traditional and really unaccepting of "alternative" lifestyles.

I suppose I did anticipate negative reactions from my parents. I believed that my siblings and friends would have positive reactions and be thrilled. I thought my parents would have to deal more with my homosexuality, if a grandchild came into existence. I didn't involve my parents in the plan. I told them of my pregnancy at the end of my first trimester.

I thought my mom would flip. Instead, she was thrilled to have another grandchild when she found out eight weeks before our daughter was born.

My mother's response when I told her I was pregnant: "Oh, great" (very sarcastically). Partner's mom (since I was the one that told her I was pregnant-partner said she couldn't do it): "I'm sorry, but I cannot say that I'm happy for you."

A sizable proportion of women did not anticipate any objections from their own families about having a child. Indeed, many of them received support and got an enthusiastic reaction from their family members.

Luckily my family is very supportive. They were relieved they would finally have grandkids.

My parents equated childlessness with being gay, so when I came out to them they were saddened (that's an understatement) for me that I wouldn't have children, as they'd always known I'd wanted.

My experience is that people will welcome a grandchild without reservation-even if the child were the spawn of the devil. Of course, my son was my parents' first grandchild. I think they had despaired of ever having a grandchild.

They were excited! Mine are the only grandchildren they have; my brother didn't want kids.

My sister is gay and she will never have a biological child, and my brother has one child. They have supported us from the beginning. My mother respects our family and accepts us as parents. I never anticipated anything negative from my family.

Gay men who were planning on having a family faced more positive responses from their own family members. In general, two-thirds of them anticipated no disapproval.

Quite the opposite. They were surprised we waited.

Our families are quite accepting of us and definitely profamily.

In fact, they were urging us to adopt-especially my mother.

We did not anticipate any negative reactions. Surprise, curiosity, etc., but nothing negative.

One-third of prospective gay fathers did anticipate disapproval from at least some members of their families over their plans.

My mother felt it would be too difficult on the children.

It turned out that they were very supportive, except my younger brother, who is gay. He wondered why any gay person would want a child.

Yes and no. I knew my parents had wanted me to have children prior to my declaration of my orientation. After my outing, I heard them express regret that I would not be giving them grandchildren. I knew that whatever means I chose to become a parent would be difficult for them to embrace as it would be different from their norm.

We had concerns. Both of our sets of parents were in their seventies, and we wondered how they would react. Also we had some concerns about some of my partner's brothers.

Gay men faced less opposition from their own families about their plans to become parents than did lesbians, perhaps because gay men and lesbians tended to choose different paths in becoming parents. Most of the gay men chose to adopt a child, and family members may have seen this as a selfless act. It is difficult to argue that taking in a child who has no family and giving that child a loving home is a selfish thing to do. On the other hand, a lesbian who elects to bring a child into the world may elicit more disapproval because others may see her decision as fulfilling her own needs, rather than a child's.

Both gay men and lesbians anticipated more disapproval from their families than they ultimately faced (see Table 7.1). While the differences were not large, it seems to be the case that lesbians and gay men who planned on becoming parents were more fearful of negative reactions from their own families than they needed to be. This suggests that, in some cases, gay men and lesbians give their own families less credit than they deserve in overcoming their homophobia, a finding that is somewhat encouraging. However, the fact remains that the initial responses from family members can be a source of stress and disappointment for prospective parents, and nearly half of the lesbians and one-quarter of the gay men in our sample did face familial disapproval.

Once the Baby Comes Home

Anticipating a birth or adoption is one thing; the arrival of a child is often something else. While many of the lesbian mothers did experience some initial disapproval from their families, often times this reaction softened with time. We did not specifically ask about how families' reactions changed once the child arrived, but some parents spontaneously wrote about the change that happened.

Initially, both set of parents were less than thrilled with the idea. Once they realized I was serious, they softened a little. And once the baby was born, they were in love with her!

My father was initially shocked, but since the baby came from me and is biologically related to him, he came around. Now he's happy to be a grandfather.

One brother-in-law had some reservations. However, he read some research on children raised in gay families on the Internet and reversed himself.

At first my partner's parents were pretty mortified. Since the kids were born, though, and since they spoke with their wonderful supportive pastor, they have almost become our biggest fans. They love the kids and us as a family.

My mom's first response when she was told: "Oh, I prayed that this is one thing you would never do." My parents have come a long way. They are now Grandpa and Grandma, and the birth of our child has made them treat my partner and me and our son as a family. They still don't tell their friends.

When we first told my parents I was actually pregnant, they both cried (not tears of joy). They were actually mad at my partner for a while. We live very close to my entire family, and we just kept being persistent about working this out. I was firm in the fact that the three of us were a family and it would be all of us or none of us. My parents contacted PFLAG [Parents and Friends of Lesbians and Gays], and by the time our daughter was born things were much better. They adore our child and treat my partner and me as a family. They are now encouraging us to have a second child.

My mother was very taken aback initially. One of my brothers was not supportive of my intentionally bringing a child into the world without a father. My mother has also expressed doubts about my being a lesbian parent. All have come around and have been fairly supportive and adore my daughter.

In some cases, however, lesbian mothers found that their families' negative feelings about their sexuality or their decision to have a child did not change even after the child was born.

My partner's father still, after twenty-five years, has never spoken to me.

My parents visit here about once a year (they live 1,300 miles away), but don't want me to visit there, since they haven't told any of their friends or neighbors about their grandchild.

My mom told me we were unfit, it wasn't right, and that I was an embarrassment to her.

In many lesbian- and gay-headed families, only one parent is biologically related to the child. Because of this, other family members may be reluctant or may refuse outright to acknowledge the nonbiological parent as a true parent.

My mom was supportive of my partner having a baby, but wanted to know when I was going to have a baby, as if her baby wouldn't be mine, or wouldn't be good enough for her.

My grandmother did get upset for a brief time. She didn't understand why I'd want to support a child that's "not mine."

Initially all family members were leery. Most have now come around (after ten years), but my dad still does not consider my nonbiological son as his grandchild.

My partner's family is fine. My mother, on the other hand, refers to my partner as "Aunt" to the children, even though I correct my mother each time it continues.

Reactions to Transracial and Other
Special Adoptions

Adoptive parents, especially those who adopted children with different racial backgrounds, often faced criticism from others on several fronts.

With our first child, both parents worried about the effect on a Black child (biracial, actually) of growing up with white lesbian parents. Both worried (aloud, in a way they wouldn't have with my heterosexual siblings) about my maturity and readiness to parent. My father was concerned that an adopted child might have genetic/emotional issues that would "make my life a living hell," and he's pretty prejudiced (he grew up in Texas). Now they adore both kids, though I'm sure they still worry. With our second, my parents worried about how hard it would be for us to have two kids, and Mom worried about "problems" she was certain would arise "down the road" as a result of our kids being raised by white lesbians.

Not because I'm a lesbian, but because I wanted to adopt an older, special-needs child.

My mom didn't think gays or lesbians were appropriate parents. I did it (took in my child) before they knew my plan. She also responded negatively to having a child of color as a grandchild. Once I was in a relationship (child #1 was about two months old) she was particularly unsupportive and didn't want my son to have my last name.

My parents advised against it. Their reasons were my age-they thought I was too old (49), and racial discrimination (my daughter is Chinese).

My mother made clear she thought I'd be a great mom. My dad had previously wanted me to "pass on my genes" and had some concerns about poor prenatal care of a child awaiting adoption.

Gay men and lesbians who choose transracial or foreign adoption are facing a double whammy. The families they are creating will have not only parents of the same gender but also parents and children from different ethnic backgrounds. Concerns about how well this unusual family will be accepted by others are common. Gay men and lesbians who are white may feel that they have a special ability to help their children deal with discrimination, as they, too, are members of a minority group.

Friends and Employers: How They Took the News

Having a child affects all domains of a parent's life. One's friends and one's employer play different yet important roles in parents' lives, and their support or lack of support significantly impacts upon prospective and new parents. The reaction of friends did not differ for the gay men and the lesbians in our sample. In both cases, fewer than one-fifth of prospective parents expected any negative reactions. However, in both cases, nearly a quarter of prospective parents did, in fact, experience some disapproval from friends (see Table 7.1). The respondents who explained this reaction indicated that some friends were unhappy with the decrease in the amount of time they would have to spend with friends, not with the fact that they had decided to have children per se.

We lost a few friends. The couldn't deal with our new priorities or time constraints.

One or two friends feared they would get less attention from me.

Surprisingly, some respondents specifically mentioned a lack of support from their lesbian friends.

I was surprised by my lesbian friends, who were not supportive in the least. My gay friends and heterosexual friends were quite supportive.

Interestingly, some lesbians responded more negatively than anyone else.

It may be that lesbians have more intimate relationships with their friends, so their lesbian friends react more negatively to the inevitable decrease in the amount of time and attention they receive from their friends who are new parents. Some lesbians may feel uncomfortable with the idea of donor insemination, which may seem too close to heterosexual intercourse, and so they cannot be supportive. It is encouraging to note that the majority (three-fourths) of our respondents received support from their friends.

Men and women had different experiences with their employers regarding their plans to become parents. Women were much more likely to anticipate difficulties; however, most of the time those difficulties never materialized (see Table 7.1). The difference in the reactions faced by men and women is clearly related to the different ways they become parents. In most of the lesbian families, one of the partners experienced pregnancy, which brought up employment-related issues such as maternity leave. Slightly more than a quarter of the lesbians were concerned about their boss's reaction to their plans for motherhood. Happily, fewer than 10 percent actually experienced any negative responses. In contrast, gay fathers, even the few who became biological parents, did not need maternity leave, and few of them expected or received any problematic responses from their employers.

Gay men and lesbians who chose to become parents tended to choose different paths and tended to receive different responses from others. Most women chose to bear their own children. Most lesbians anticipated negative reactions from their own families, and, while positive experiences were more common than they expected, nearly half did, in fact, experience some opposition to their plans. A quarter of them worried that they would experience some employment-related problems, though, again, fewer than 10 percent actually experienced such difficulties. Gay men who wished to become parents, on the other hand, generally chose to adopt. Most of them did not expect any resistance from their own families regarding their plans, and few encountered any. A sizable minority of both groups experienced some lack of support from their friends, including gay and lesbian friends.

The level of social support that prospective gay and lesbian parents receive is one that may have far-reaching implications. For example, it has been found that the more social support a woman receives during pregnancy, the greater her psychological well-being, fewer complications, and even more positive birth outcomes (Dunkel-Schetter, Sagrestano, Feldman, & Killingsworth, 1996). It may be that those lesbians who experience little support from others, or even downright disapproval, may be at risk for developing problems during pregnancy. Social support, through its impact upon the parents' emotional well-being may also affect parental behavior (Simons & Johnson, 1996). Our results suggested that in most cases the disapproval, particularly from family members, was transitory. The short- and long-term implications of lack of social support, as well as gay and lesbian parents' methods of coping with this lack, need to be addressed.

Putting the Plan into Action: How Hard Is It for Gay and Lesbian Parents to Adopt or Become Pregnant?

In most cases, the answer is it is not hard for gay and lesbian parents to adopt or to become pregnant. That is, most prospective parents do not anticipate any resistance from fertility clinics, gynecologists, or adoption agencies to their wish to become parents, and most do not meet any resistance. Among lesbian mothers, 26 percent anticipated at least some difficulty from medical care providers or adoption agencies, while only 11 percent actually experienced any difficulties. Of gay fathers, 20 percent thought they would be given a hard time, which turned out to be an accurate assessment. The majority of gay and lesbian parents found acceptance, from the staff at fertility clinics to the adoption professionals up to the labor and delivery team.

When we went to the hospital we had written a birth plan. It explained our family and that we would all be involved. We passed it out to the hospital staff. [from a mother of a family that includes two moms and two dads]

We used a nurse midwife. They were great. We attended every pre-natal visit together and the childbirth and breastfeeding classes to-gether. The hospital staff was great.

As our results suggest, some anticipated difficulties never materialized, and parents were pleasantly surprised at the acceptance they found.

We thought the medical profession would be biased against us. Perhaps we would be considered unfit. But everyone was great-very open and kind. Many were openly curious and asked well-intended questions.

I was apprehensive about medical care-having to come out and possibly face resistance to inseminating in the doctor's office. But my gynecologist was great, as were the fertility specialists and all staff involved. The obstetricians were equally wonderful. Everyone was so supportive. Some of them related stories about gay family members.

We expected some difficulties finding birth mothers who would agree to place their child in a gay family, but we were surprised how many birth mothers were willing to do this.

As stated, some individuals did encounter negative responses or outright rejection from professionals in the medical or adoption fields. While there are no laws that expressly prohibit a doctor from inseminating an unmarried woman, for example, some doctors refuse to do so. Some states prohibit gay men and lesbians from adopting a child, and, even in states that do not do so, some private agencies may choose to handle only married heterosexual clients.

Initially I had a hard time finding a doctor who would inseminate me as a single women. I didn't reveal my lesbianism. After our first son was born, we attempted adoption as a lesbian family and had many doors slammed.

Some women decided to bypass the doctor or fertility clinic entirely and did inseminations on their own or with the help of their partner. Some sperm banks deliver sperm directly to patients' homes; other prospective parents picked up the semen samples themselves from the sperm banks. Home inseminations are not difficult, and some clinics or doctors give patients instructions on how they are done.

The first program that helped us save our first donor's semen later developed a policy in which they would only agree to treat married heterosexual couples. For our second child I had my own cryotank [container in which frozen sperm is kept] and I did my own "infertility" work for my partner.

I had several doctors say they could not help me become pregnant because I was single.

No agencies would work with us when we adopted. We were told that our only option was to find a pregnant mother to choose us and to work with an attorney.

Our findings suggest that many, if not most, current physicians have few problems in dealing with gay or lesbian parents. Adoption agencies, for the most part, are also quite willing to help gay men and lesbians achieve parenthood and often assist them in circumventing prohibitions against gay adoption (by referring to the adoptive parent's partner as a "roommate" on the home study, even though the agency knows the real situation, for example). Interestingly, lesbians anticipated more difficulty than they actually found as they began to work toward parenthood. Gay men were more likely to encounter resistance from professionals in their quest for parenthood. This is the opposite of the pattern we found when looking at family reactions, which showed that lesbians encountered more disapproval. Again, we suggest that the difference probably results from the different methods gay men and lesbians use in becoming parents. Most lesbian families are created through donor insemination. There are no laws prohibiting insemination of lesbians. On the other hand, most gay fathers become fathers through adoption, and some states expressly forbid homosexuals from adopting. Foreign adoptions are generally not open to homosexuals, either, and to go through a foreign adoption one of the parents must be presented as a single parent. It seems that the gay men in our sample were quite accurate in their assessment of the opposition they would face.

Coming Out Comes after Children: Families Begun in Heterosexual Relationships

Approximately one-third of the families in our study had begun within heterosexual relationships. Interestingly, there were no blended families among the male-headed families; that is, there were no cases where there were some children in the family who had been born or adopted into a heterosexual relationship and some who had been born or adopted into the gay relationship. In contrast, there were sixteen such families among the lesbian-headed families. The couples in the blended lesbian families had been together on average nearly eight years, while the couples in the stepfamilies (who had no children together) had been together an average of just under three and a half years. Some of the stepfamilies mentioned that they hoped to have a child together in the future. Lesbian couples, more than gay male couples, are likely to add to their existing families. Again, the relative ease with which lesbians can have children must be a factor in their increased likelihood to form blended families.

We limited participation in this study to parents who were currently living with their children, so the parents in the gay and lesbian stepfamilies all had custody of their children. We did not ask specifically about the custody decision, but some parents offered information about it.

My divorce was extremely difficult. My ex-husband had just "found God" and said many negative things about me in court. He testified (with others from his church) that homosexuals are unfit to be parents. In the end, the judge ruled that who I choose to love does not reflect upon my abilities as a parent. I won sole custody.

When my child got involved in the court system at one point, the judge ordered counseling for our daughter as "having gay parents must bother her."

My son's father had concerns very early on about how my relationship would affect our son. I told him that it wouldn't make him any different, and I never heard anything else from him about the subject.

As a rule, courts are less inclined to consider a parent's sexuality when making custody decisions than they used to be. Of course, individual judges may be predisposed to view homosexuality as incompatible with parenthood, and gay and lesbian parents cannot assume that their sexuality will be viewed as irrelevant. Still, the legal climate for gay and lesbian parents is generally improving.

These couples began their relationship with a child already present. As one mother put it:

My daughter was almost two when we started living together. My daughter and I were a package deal for my girlfriend.

Beginning a relationship with someone who is already a parent sometimes has unanticipated repercussions.

I never realized when I partnered with the kids' mom that I'd acquire an "ex-husband"-and his fiancée. It's not bad, just something I never thought about.

Everyone I work with knows that I am the parent of two children. They all know that, even though I am not the biological parent, I regard the children as my own. I am often told that I am a great person for taking this role on. I myself disagree. I don't think it's anything to "take on." It just so happened that I fell in love with a woman that has two kids.

My son outed me to his preschool. His friends were asking me if my son had any brothers or sisters and when I answered no, he said he had "a mommy, a daddy, and a Barbara." It was all perfectly natural to him.

The stepfamilies in our sample differed from the primary gay and lesbian families in how long they had been together and in how old their children were (on average), as well as in the circumstances under which they formed their families. In the remaining chapters, we look at the functioning of these families more closely.

[PART TWO]

[8]

Gay and Lesbian Parents' Beliefs about Parenting

All parents have concerns about their children, goals they wish to strive for as parents, and experiences they feel are important for their children to have. We asked our subjects about these issues in order to see how gay and lesbian parents view their priorities as parents. We deliberately asked the questions in an open-ended manner so that the respondents could interpret them and answer them in their own ways. We were interested in seeing whether more participants cited concerns having to do with the dynamics of their families or with the greater community in which they lived. In other words, we wanted to know whether gay and lesbian parents are more concerned about themselves as parents or about society's reaction to their family? Are their goals and objectives as parents influenced greatly by their sexual orientation, or are they similar to the goals and objectives of most heterosexual parents?

Concerns about Raising Children in Gay- or Lesbian-Headed Families

Most of the parents admitted to having particular concerns about raising a child in a gay- or lesbian-headed family. Eighty-one percent of the lesbian mothers indicated that they felt this way, as did 73 percent of gay fathers. When asked to name their specific concerns, 85 percent of the fathers and 82 percent of the mothers who had concerns said they worried that their children would be teased by other children because of their family makeup.

I fear that my child may be harassed by schoolmates. I don't know of any other gay/lesbian parents in my community. I don't want her to feel embarrassed.

My concerns mainly are about any negative words or actions that may be taken against my children because their parents are lesbian (teasing, fighting, etc.). So far that hasn't happened, but they are still too young.

I do worry about the reaction our son will face throughout life without a mother actively raising him. No matter what we do to prepare him for his, someone sometime will be negative or cruel to him about having two dads.

Seventeen percent of lesbian mothers with concerns and 8 percent of gay fathers with concerns cited the lack of a role model for one gender in the family as something they worried about. (Note that, because some parents mentioned more than one concern, totals may add up to more than 100 percent.)

I want to ensure my children have access to positive male role models.

At first I worried about the absence of a male parent, but after reading *The Courage to Raise Good Men* I was much less anxious and now believe we can raise healthy, good kids.

We're a little concerned about making sure that our daughter had good male role models like her daddy and papa (she has two gay dads, too.)

Will we [two gay fathers] be able to teach our daughter the essentials of womanhood?

Other concerns came up more rarely. Many of these concerns were variations on the theme of how others will perceive the child. Some dealt with the implications of having used an unknown donor or being unable to obtain legal rights as a parent. Some parents did express worries about their own parenting and its potential impact upon their children.

I have had some concerns that our son, with two fathers, have good role models of heterosexual intimacy and friendship.

I do have custody concerns if my partner and I should split, since I don't have much protection here in our state. [from a nonbiological lesbian mother]

I was raised without a biological dad. I had a hard time with the concept of doing the same to another child.

I fear that he will resent us for using an unknown donor. He can never know who the donor is.

How do we encourage truth if we can't be open about our lifestyle choices everyday? [this lesbian mother is a teacher at a Catholic school, and would lose her job if her sexual orientation were to become known, so she is in the closet professionally]

Our son tends to enjoy "girl" things (Barbies, playing "dress-up"-with dresses). We're afraid that he'll be taunted (more than kids usually are) and that we'll be accused of coercing or leading him into a "gay" life.

I have been concerned that gay/lesbian relationships are often not long term and that our daughter may experience too much loss as partners come and go from our lives. [from a single lesbian mother who is coparenting with a single gay father]

I am worried that they may reject me when they are older (as the adoptive, not the "real," parent). [from a nonbiological lesbian mother]

Advantages of Growing Up in Gay- or Lesbian-Headed Families

Most of the parents also felt that their children would gain some particular advantages as a result of living in a gay- or lesbian-headed family. Specifically, 89 percent of lesbian mothers and 82 percent of gay fathers felt that their children would benefit in some way from having grown up in their particular families. This is congruent with Harris & Turner's (1986) findings that lesbian mothers perceive more advantage for their children in their household makeup than do gay fathers.

The most commonly mentioned advantage was the belief that the experience of growing up in a family that is perceived as "different" would make their children more accepting of differences in others. Fifty-four percent of mothers and 63 percent of fathers who saw advantages felt that their children would grow up more tolerant and less prejudiced as a result of having gay or lesbian parents.

I think they grow up with a better understanding about differences in people and in families and are better able to appreciate these differences.

They are in a very unique situation: They're Jewish Chinese vegetarians, who speak Hebrew at home and have two daddies. This gives them a unique perspective on life, and an automatic openness.

We are perhaps more aware of how people treat others who are different and this will lead to more compassion for others.

The second most commonly named advantage of raising children in a gay or lesbian home was cited by parents who had begun their families within the context of a gay or lesbian relationship. Many of these parents (32 percent of mothers and 20 percent of fathers) felt that, since gays and lesbians have to surmount so many obstacles in having children, this makes them more appreciative and loving parents.

She [her daughter] was more planned and wanted than many children born of straight couples.

I think raising a child by two loving moms is the best possible situation. Females tend to be more attentive and openly expressive of love and caring. What is better than two?!

First, we had to do a lot of soul searching before we decided to have a child, so I think he'll benefit from how we had to think everything through. Plus, he is very much a wanted child.

Some parents (8 percent of mothers and 5 percent of fathers) felt that children raised in a gay or lesbian home would be exposed to more equal parenting and hence develop less stereotypical ideas of how men and women should behave.

I think it is good for my son to see all kinds of projects and chores done by women. Everything from cleaning to mowing to car repair is done by his moms, and I think it is good that he doesn't have a certain gender assigned to certain types of chores.

We do less gender-specific role modeling. Our boys are able to express a greater range of feeling. They can be nurturing and physically affectionate.

The lesbian and gay families we know seem to have more egalitarian roles in raising children than our heterosexual counterparts.

He will see males being nurturing and domestic.

Other perceived advantages were mentioned infrequently but provided an interesting look at how some gay and lesbian parents see themselves and their families.

We are providing the basic message that the most important thing in life is to follow our heart and your convictions, which will provide internal peace, rather than simply trying to be like everyone else.

We were able to get our son into any private school we wanted-since they were all interested in having gay dads for parents.

I see an advantage if our son turns out to be gay. I think it will be easier for him to come out and accept himself.

We are very strong emotionally by virtue of facing our homosexuality in the face of societal condemnation. Our children will grow up knowing tolerance and aware they can be who they feel themselves to be, without fear of our disapproval.

Our child benefits from the lesbian community's ethic of helping one another. Straight families have been amazed by the level of community support we enjoy in raising our child.

The kids know we are together because we love each other, not by marriage, making choice a powerful force. They are more aware of legal inequities and more open-minded that anyone can love anyone.

Gay and lesbian parents are well aware of the social difficulties that their children may face because of them. Their biggest concern centers around the possibility that other children will tease or make fun of their child for having "queer" parents. Interestingly, although the absence of a role model of the opposite sex is often cited as a problem in gay and lesbian families, only a few of gay and lesbian parents themselves were concerned about this. It seems that what concerns gay and lesbian parents the most is not anything related to the dynamics of the family but, rather, the outside community's reactions. We conclude from this that, for most gay and lesbian parents, the greatest apprehension concerns not how well they do their job as parents but how society will treat their children because of them.

At the same time, gay and lesbian parents feel that their children will receive important benefits from having been raised by them-specifically, that their children will be more tolerant and accepting individuals. Their responses seem to suggest that the experience of growing up in a family that is labeled "different," coupled with parents' specific teaching about respecting others, will lead their children in this direction. There are some data that support this idea. Saffron (1998) interviewed seventeen British adolescents and young adults who had grown up with lesbian mothers. She found that the children themselves felt they had benefitted from having a lesbian mother, in that they were more aware of prejudice and more accepting of diversity. This suggests that gay and lesbian parents may be correct: Their children may well be more tolerant and broadminded.

Aspirations of Gay and Lesbian Parents

We asked the parents in our study to list three values they felt were most important to instill in their children. We were interested in hearing from gay and lesbian parents themselves about their goals for their children and their priorities as parents. We found that their responses could easily be classified into a small number of categories. The most frequently cited trait gay and lesbian parents wanted to instill in their children is a respect for others and tolerance for diversity. This wish, that their children would grow up free from prejudice and valuing all others equally, was mentioned by two-thirds of the respondents.

The next most commonly cited goal was to instill self-respect in their children. More than half of the parents mentioned the importance of promoting high self-esteem, confidence, and self-assurance in their children. The third most commonly mentioned trait was a strong moral code. Just under half the parents said that they felt that instilling moral qualities such as honesty, integrity, and good values was most important. The five most frequently mentioned traits are listed in Table 8.1.

TABLE 8.1

What Parents Want to Instill in Their Children

Goal	Number of times cited
Teach respect for others	272
Instill as sense of self-esteem	264
Instill a sense of values and honesty	213
Provide security, unconditional love	81
Foster a positive outlook	59

NOTE: Parents could list up to three traits. Some listed one or two. The five most frequently cited responses are given here.

It appears that gay and lesbian parents value teaching their children to respect others, in particular others who are different from them. The reason for this may be that the parents have felt what it is like to experience discrimination and bigotry from other people, and they want to make sure that their children do not treat others that way. It may also be that, by teaching their children about discrimination, they are in effect inoculating them against the homophobia they will inevitably encounter. As we have seen, gay and lesbian parents' greatest concern is that their children will be teased. With this in mind, their emphasis on teaching their children that it is wrong to treat others unkindly because they are different may, in part, be an effort to help their children put teasing into perspective. They show their children examples of racism or other kinds of discrimination so that their children will recognize homophobia for what it is—an unjust mistreatment of a minority group. Teaching children to respect others and to appreciate tolerance is a noble goal for any parent, but it may also include a bit of self-interest for the gay or lesbian parent.

We asked the parents to think back to their own childhoods and to list up to three things that they would like to do the same as their parents did. (See Table 8.2.) We were interested in seeing how they viewed their experiences with their own families as they were growing up and how these experiences affect their own behavior as parents. Their responses tended to center around two areas: emphasizing the importance of education and family closeness.

We also asked parents to think about their own childhood experiences and to list up to three things that they would like to do differently from their parents. (See Table 8.3.) The single most common area in which gay and lesbian parents want to improve, as compared to their own parents, is in the area of discipline. Many parents spoke about wanting to avoid using physical punishment with their own children. The other

TABLE 8.2
What Parents Want to Do the Same as Their Parents

Goal	Number of times cited
Emphasize education, cultural experiences	136
Give unconditional love	131
Spend family time	125
Instill self-esteem	107
Encourage values, honesty	96

NOTE: Parents could list up to three traits. Some listed one or two. The five most commonly cited are given here.

TABLE 8.3

What Parents Want to Do Differently from Their Own Parents

Goal	Number of times cited
Be a better disciplinarian	168
Instill self-esteem	115
Emphasize education, cultural experiences	91
Give security, unconditional love	89
Spend family time	76

NOTE: Parents could list up to three traits. Some listed one or two. The five most frequently cited responses are given here.

most frequently cited domains where gay and lesbian parents wanted to do better than their parents were in inculcating a strong sense of self, encouraging educational experiences, and giving their children affection and love.

When asked about what they would do the same as their parents and what they would like to do differently, gay fathers and lesbian mothers sound like any other mothers and fathers. There is nothing striking in their responses that differs from what one would expect the responses of parents of young children to be. All parents have to deal with issues of maintaining discipline, instilling values, encouraging achievement, and maintaining closeness. Gay and lesbian parents are not interested only in how their sexual orientation impacts upon their children, although they certainly are interested in that. They are also interested in providing their children with the most supportive and encouraging environment they can. They are focused on many things-education, close family ties, high self-esteem-that have nothing to do with their own sexuality. These findings underscore that gay and lesbian parents are in many ways just like other parents.

Gay and lesbian parents find many things that they wish to reproduce from their childhoods. At the same time, they are also able to identify things that they do not want to repeat with their own children. They want to encourage their children to be educated, cultured individuals, with a strong sense of self and a love for their family. They want to discipline their children in a more effective manner. They want their children to grow up with a respect for other people and their differences and to display integrity and responsibility when dealing with others.

How do Professionals Treat Gay and Lesbian Families?

Openness with Family Doctors

Given that gay and lesbian parents showed such concern about other people's reactions to their families, we were interested in exploring how open they were with other people about their families. We asked about their openness with the two groups of professionals who have the most contact with their children: their child's doctor and their child's teacher or daycare provider. We felt that their openness, or secrecy, regarding their family is an important indicator of their approach to the outside world. We also believe that the way in which they talk about their families, or don't talk about their families, sends a message to their children about how they expect to be treated.

The overwhelming majority of gay and lesbian parents were open about being gay or lesbian parents with their children's doctor. Overall, 83 percent of lesbian mothers and 79 percent of gay fathers had spoken to their children's pediatrician or family doctor about their family makeup. Many parents had interviewed prospective pediatricians, some even before the birth of their child, in order to find one who would be open and accepting of their family.

We screened for a gay-friendly pediatrician. Got lucky with our first interview. He already had another set of lesbian parents (for whose second parent adoption he wrote a letter of support. Later he did the same for us.) Our pediatrician has a generally diverse clientele. He's totally supportive of our right to live as we choose.

We chose our pediatrician with an interview before our son was born and simply showed ourselves as a family. We were supported and the pediatrician did not respond in any particular way. She is open and respectful and supportive of our family-involves us equally as moms.

When we interviewed the pediatricians available under my health insurance, we made it clear we were a lesbian couple and that that fact not only had to be OK with the doctor, it had to be acknowledged and valued by the doctor. We went with the pediatrician who best exemplified this. The first one we interviewed made a point of saying our relationship was OK (and our response was "Yes it is, but we want more than that."). The one we went with said only that she had other lesbian parents in the practice and thought they were great-and went on to talk about her medical philosophy, not about us.

Some parents, while being open about their family, were less proactive in their approach, either waiting to be asked or presenting themselves as a family without any lengthy explanation. We felt that this was a stylistic difference but that it had the same ultimate effect of being open and out about the family structure.

We just let them figure it out. When they asked "Who is Mommy?" we said, "We are." They responded most notably by not responding. Some were uncomfortable, but they kept their doctor/nurse face and persevered. It's turned out OK.

At the first visit to the pediatrician, we were asked what the social situation was at home, and we then explained. The doctor rolled right with it and shared that he had a professor in his residency last year who had done the same thing and he thought it was cool.

Initially with the first son we were not open as a lesbian family, and my partner and I referred to each other as coparents to our son. That was awkward and uncomfortable for us and confusing to them. As we became more confident in our parenting role (about six months), we dropped this charade and have been addressing medical care providers as a lesbian family and that our children have two moms, both of whom can make any medical decisions, instead.

Some parents volunteered that they did encounter negative responses from medical professionals. These responses ranged from a slight feeling of awkwardness or discomfort to outright rejection.

The pediatrician who circumcised our son at the hospital could only talk to the bio-mother. He couldn't explain to me how to care for my son after the surgery until I promised him that he'd never see us again. Our pediatrician in our town was fantastic, but when we moved to another town, one pediatrician refused to see us because of our "situation."

Sometimes the doctor will act like it is a big deal to care for my child. And when one of my boys talks about his gay dad, most of our doctors have a disgusted look on their face.

The fact that the majority of parents in our study were open with their children's pediatricians or family doctors suggests that gay and lesbian parents take a frank, forthright approach to dealing with the medical profession. The parents' responses generally reflected a thoughtful approach to broaching the topic with doctors. While we did not specifically ask about their ongoing relationship with the doctor or health professional, most parents indicated that they felt comfortable and pleased with their treatment by the medical community.

Openness with Teachers

Teachers are very important people in children's lives. Most gay and lesbian parents feel it is important to let teachers, daycare providers, and other caregivers know about their family situation. The overwhelming majority of the lesbian mothers and gay fathers in our study are open with their child's teacher. Among those parents who started their families within a gay or lesbian relationship, 80 percent of mothers and 93 percent of fathers did disclose their status as gay parents to the child's teacher. (This figure may be a bit misleading for lesbian mothers: 13 percent of them had children who were too young for school.)

Many of the parents were fortunate enough to have been able to place their children in schools that already have other gay or lesbian families enrolled. For these families, this was an important factor in their choosing a school.

We've always thought it was important. Her first teacher was lesbian too. The school (we feel too guilty when we call it daycare) is eclectic and very open to alternative families, so we've never had any problem.

We're open to the daycare provider; in fact, that was a screening question in selecting the provider. We are not the first gay family she has encountered, either.

Even in situations where there were no other children of gay or lesbian parents, few parents report any problems with teachers or schools.

We volunteered this information because we believe it is in our children's best interest. We were apprehensive because we live in a conservative suburb in the heart of the "Bible Belt." However, we have been extremely pleased with the response of teachers and school counselors. So far, all have taken the news in stride. It's almost a nonissue.

We have been completely out and open with our son's preschool teachers. We volunteered that information prior to enrolling him, and they said they had no problem with that because they are infinitely more interested in kids than they are in parents!

We volunteered the information-first on school forms on which we indicated our child has two mothers, then by introducing ourselves to teachers at school functions. If they were surprised, they covered it and then demonstrated positive support. Our daughter's kindergarten teacher last year recently made a point of thanking me for "opening up her eyes." (I'm not sure quite what she meant, but her response was so enthusiastic I could only assume it was positive!)

His daycare provider was very supportive of us. She was motherly at first-giving us tips and reminders, pointing things out. She realized we were open to help, yet very loving dads. We are still close to the provider and her husband. His preschool is wonderful. We are active in the center and supportive of their program. They are open-call us by family names of "Dad" and "Popper." We are very pleased.

A number of parents made a distinction between letting their child's teacher know that their child has two parents of the same gender and spelling out to the teacher what that implies about the parents' sexuality.

We just let her [nanny employed in the home] assume what she will. We are "Mommy" and "Mama" to our son, and she used those in reference to us. She never asked [about our sexuality], but we never volunteered. We just try to act like we are normal and hope others will follow our lead.

We generally present ourselves as a "visual display" (described as two moms) early in the school year. We don't tend to lead off with the "L" word, but haven't avoided it.

In a small number of cases, parents who have made a point of being open with childcare providers have found their openness met with rejection.

When it became evident to the first daycare we had our son in that, yes, indeed, we were a lesbian family, the "Christian" daycare asked us to remove our four-month-old son.

Single women, or those who had their children while in heterosexual relationships, were less likely to be open about their lesbianism with their children's teachers. As these comments from formerly married women suggest, a common strategy is to let people surmise what they want to.

It has not come up. Most people assume I am a divorced single mother living with a friend.

It hasn't come up directly, but they know her daddy and I are divorced, and they also know that another woman who lives with Mommy picks up my child and takes her to school.

We informed his teacher that my partner lives with us and is involved in his activities and education. I didn't think she needed to know the exact nature of our relationship, although she probably did know. I also didn't want to cause problems for our son at this point in time. He is only in first grade, and I didn't think he was ready to deal with it.

As a group, women who had had their children during heterosexual relationships were less likely to be open about being lesbian mothers than were those who had had their children within the lesbian relationship, perhaps because, for many of them, the lesbian relationship is still relatively new, and they are being cautious about letting other people know about it. In some cases, the new partner may not yet have taken on a parental role with the children, so the biological mother feels it is not necessary for the child's teacher to know about the situation. Still, 61 percent of the formerly married women who were currently in relationships with women did let their children's teachers know about their new families.

From the start of my partner's and my relationship, we made it a point to make it know and be up front yet casual about it. We haven't experienced any problems so far.

We were open with teachers. Most were OK; one or two kind of stepped back a bit.

Yes, his teacher is aware because she needs to know in case of an emergency at school. If he talks about us, they need to know how to handle the other kids and how much they can explain to the other kids if they have questions.

It hasn't been an issue. Teachers call and ask for either of us by name. In the student directory, I am listed as "parent" to both kids. The response has been, to my surprise, very good. I expected it to be difficult and to be denied the privilege of attending conferences and so on.

Another factor that is related to how open parents are with teachers is the age of the child. As children get older, some parents feel it is less important that each teacher know about their families.

At different ages I have handled it different ways, and each year I have to decide what to do again. In sixth grade I told my daughter's teachers, and she was very angry at me for doing so. She did not want to be identified as different in that way.

I have not directly told teachers, especially during middle school years, mostly due to my daughter's request. But my partner and I attend conferences, school, and athletic functions together. The response has been fine. [from a lesbian mother who was single for much of her daughter's life]

Gay and lesbian parents are, for the most part, open about their families with their children's health care providers and with their teachers. Their responses indicate that not only do they want these influential people to be aware of their family circumstances but they also make a point of letting them know that they are gay or lesbian parents. The data indicate that the respondents feel very strongly about presenting themselves as out and as proud gay or lesbian families to the professionals who play important roles in their children's lives.

Openness with Other People in the Children's Lives

As children get older, their social worlds expand. They start choosing their own friends, becoming involved in extracurricular activities, and developing their own social networks. This means that parents must interact with a host of new people who are now in their children's lives: sports coaches, ballet teachers, scout troop leaders, and other parents. In these more informal situations, again we find that most gay and lesbian parents are open about their families. (See Table 8.4.) The pattern that we found before emerged once again, with parents who had their children within the gay or lesbian relationship being more open about their families than those who had their children while in a heterosexual relationship.

Many parents mentioned making a conscious decision as to how to broach the topic of their own family with other people. A strategy often mentioned was to let people get to know them a little bit before discussing their family situation. Another frequently cited approach was to explain that the child has two mothers or two fathers and to let the implications of that statement speak for themselves.

TABLE 8.4

Families' Openness with Others

	Child's Friends' Parents	Extracurricular Coaches
WOMEN		
Primary lesbian	73 (67%)	51 (50%)
Lesbian stepfamilies	33 (47%)	22 (41%)
MEN		
Primary gay	27 (90%)	20 (71%)
Gay stepfamilies	8 (33%)	4 (24%)

Yes, we are open, but we are more subtle about it. We don't hide anything, but we feel it helps if the parents can get to know us a little before we jump right in. So far we have not encountered any negative reactions.

We have been open-although it's also pretty obvious. We don't always say the "L" word at our first meeting, because it seems to have too high a shock quotient. We just say "Annie has two moms" and move on. I avoid talking about my partner or our relationship the first few times we meet. But if the relationship continues, then I talk, and there hasn't been any problem.

At this point, our oldest is three. He hasn't had much opportunity to make friends without us around. We have been more or less open in his YMCA classes and music classes, simply by both attending or introducing ourselves as his two moms. I guess we leave the deduction of sexuality to their imagination. Usually the first response is surprise, as that's not what they expect, but generally it doesn't make much difference to them.

When the questions arise regarding "mother," we say our child has a papa and a daddy. I wait mostly to be asked, only because no one else is volunteering their particular situation. I don't feel people present themselves as a sexual orientation upon meeting. If my partner and I are together, I present us as a couple.

Some parents make it a point to be as out as possible as early as possible with everyone, and to use the "G" or "L" word specifically.

We have been completely out and open and have volunteered the details of our situation to our child's friends' parents. No negative reactions thus far. Most people just seem curious about how our family came about.

We are totally out and open. It has always been important to present ourselves as a proud, normal family. No problems.

My children's friends knew and liked me before, so now they know and like a lesbian. [from a lesbian mother who was formerly in a heterosexual marriage]

Some formerly heterosexual parents allow a certain amount of mystery regarding their current situation to exist among other people.

Our eleven-year-old brings one friend around. His mom has talked on the phone to my partner and in person to me. I'm not sure if she knows we're two different people.

No, friends' parents weren't told. But they do know that I live with a woman. I don't think they put two and two together because we each have a child.

Our son played baseball for the first time this year and is currently taking swimming lessons. This issue really hasn't come up, although

I think we have confused some of the parents, since my partner and I both take him to activities. Nobody has asked, and we have not volunteered the information.

We pick and choose on this issue. Mostly, it just doesn't come up. Sometimes we choose not to share the nature of our relationship voluntarily, but would not lie about it if asked directly by the parents of one of our children's friends. Those who know seem to be OK with it. As far as we know, none of our children has been "dropped" by a friend due to our relationship.

It is clear that most gay and lesbian parents are not living in the closet but are open about themselves and their families within the communities in which they live. Their approach to dealing with other people in general is similar to their way of dealing with professionals: Most are open. The majority of these parents do not live in large urban areas, so it is not the case that all of these families are living in a few progressive cities with large gay populations. Once again, parents who lived in gay or lesbian stepfamilies were somewhat more selective in sharing the details of their lives. We suspect that two things are going on with these families. First, they are going through a process of establishing a family, which entails working out both the couple relationship and the stepparent-child relationship. Family members may be reluctant to disclose the nature of their relationship before they are sure about it themselves. Second, the children in these families are older than the children in the primary gay or lesbian families, and they are beginning to have more involvement in the decision about disclosure. It is also striking that few parents mention having had negative responses from others. It seems, to judge from this sample, that gay and lesbian parents are joining the larger population of parents in areas all over the country and are doing so with relative ease.

[9]

Life within Gay and Lesbian Families

Who Does What?

Raising children and maintaining a household are never-ending tasks. Research on heterosexual parents has found that the manner in which couples share these responsibilities influences how satisfied they are with their relationship, and this in turn influences their parenting (see Chapter 1 for a fuller discussion of these issues). Heterosexual parents tend to fall back on traditional gender roles once they have children, with the mother assuming the role of the primary nurturer and caretaker for the children. Even when both parents are employed and both desire a more equal parenting arrangement, heterosexual mothers still take on most of the responsibilities at home (Hochschild, 1989).

Among gay or lesbian couples, there is no automatic gender-related assumption that one partner will have most of the responsibility for running the household and taking care of the children. Couples made up of two women or two men may elect to fall back upon a traditional division of labor, with one partner assuming the traditional "masculine" role and the other the traditional "feminine" role, or they may decide to divide tasks more equitably, according to interests and abilities. Some research has shown that, in general, gay and lesbian couples are more egalitarian in their division of labor (Blumstein & Schwartz, 1983; Kurdek, 1993). For heterosexual couples, however, the time when roles become most gender specific is once they have children (Cowan & Cowan, 1992). Do gay and lesbian couples, once they become parents, tend to show a traditional division of labor, or do they maintain their relatively egalitarian division? Previous studies suggest that, most of the time, they maintain their egalitarian approach. Compared with heterosexual parents, for example, lesbian parents show more equal participation in parenting. Lesbian nonbiological mothers have been found to be more involved in the daily responsibilities of childcare than heterosexual fathers (Tasker & Golombok, 1998). Sullivan (1996) found that the majority of lesbian couples with children in her study (twenty-nine out of thirty-four) apportioned their employment, childcare, and household work in an egalitarian manner. Patterson (1995a) also found, in her examination of twenty-nine families, that lesbian couples generally divide tasks in a fairly egalitarian manner; however, in primary lesbian families, the biological mother tends to do more of the childcare. We were interested in examining the pattern of dividing tasks in our sample of parents.

We asked those parents who are currently in a relationship to rate their division of labor in two areas: their housekeeping tasks and their child-rearing responsibilities. Agreement between partners was very strong, with both partners seeming to view things the same way. (See Table 9.1.) These

TABLE 9.1

Interpartner Agreement on Division of Labor

	Housekeeping	Child Rearing
WOMEN		
Primary lesbian	.68***	.67***
Lesbian stepfamilies	.70***	.56***
MEN		
Primary gay	.74***	.80***

NOTE: There were too few male couples whose children had been conceived in a prior heterosexual relationship to include in the analyses.

*** ≤ .001

correlations are comparable to those found in studies of heterosexual couples with children (see Deal, Hagan, and Anderson, 1992, for example). This suggests that gay and lesbian parents, like heterosexual parents, agree with each others' estimations about how much of the workload each one carries.

Overall, very few couples reported that one partner took on all or most of the responsibilities associated with maintaining a household or taking care of children. In fact, the parents in this study generally describe a very egalitarian arrangement. Fifty percent of the respondents answered the question about who does the bulk of the childcare with a score of "4", meaning "We share equally"; 49 percent gave that response to the question about household tasks. As a group, these parents report an evenly balanced picture of family life, with both parents taking on a roughly similar amount of responsibility (see Table 9.2).

TABLE 9.2

Percentage of Mothers Who Report Taking Equal Responsibility

	Housekeeping	Child Rearing
Biological Mothers		
Primary lesbian	47%	62%
Lesbian stepfamilies	58%	42%

Even within families where the workload is fairly evenly divided, there can still be differences between partners. Other research on lesbian couples (Patterson, 1995a) has found that, among families where the child had been born into the lesbian relationship, biological mothers tend to do more of the child-rearing tasks than do nonbiological mothers. This difference existed among Patterson's subjects even though the partners' division of the workload was relatively even. We were interested in seeing whether the same pattern would show up in our research. We were also interested in seeing whether the same pattern would exist among the formerly heterosexual subjects in our study, those who had brought their children into new relationships. We also wanted to explore the division of labor among gay fathers, which has not been studied before.

We did, in fact, find the same pattern that other research has found among lesbian parents (see Tables 9.3 and 9.4). In those families that had begun within the lesbian relationship, biological mothers did take on more of the responsibilities for childcare. And, as in the previous study, the difference for household tasks approached significance. It may be that in

TABLE 9.3

Division of Labor among Mothers in Primary Lesbian Families

	Biological Mother	Nonbiological	Mother t-Test
HOUSEKEEPING			
Mean	3.65[1]	3.97	1.87+
Standard deviation	1.03	0.88	
CHILD REARING			
Mean	3.76	4.17	3.17**
Standard deviation	0.75	0.74	

NOTE: In this analysis, those families where both mothers had given birth to a child were excluded. Sixty-six biological mothers were included. Sixty-five nonbiological mothers answered the question on childcare responsibilities, and sixty-three answered the household tasks questions.

[1] 1 = I do it all; 4 = We share equally; 7 = My partner does it all; +p < .10; **p ≤ .01

TABLE 9.4

Division of Labor among Mothers in Lesbian Stepfamilies

	Biological Mother	Nonbiological	Mother t-Test
HOUSEKEEPING			
Mean	3.88[1]	4.18	1.41
Standard deviation	0.93	0.81	
CHILD REARING			
Mean	3.51	4.45	3.40***
Standard deviation	1.22	1.00	

NOTE: Thirty-three couples were included in this analysis.

[1] 1 = I do it all; 4 = We share equally; 7 = My partner does it all; ***p ≤ .001

lesbian couples, the tendency is for biological mothers to devote more time to childcare tasks and for nonbiological mothers to spend more time in paid employment, as Patterson found. In fact, we found a similar tendency in our sample. Among the primary lesbian families, the biological mothers spent an average of thirty-five hours per week in paid employment, while the nonbiological mothers worked forty hours per week, on average. This is not a striking difference, but it may account for the biological mothers' slight propensity to do more of the childcare. This pattern may begin when the children are infants, if the biological mother has maternity leave and thus more time to spend with the child. Among lesbian couples who brought the child into the relationship with them, the biological mothers also did more of the childcare work. There was a tendency for the biological mothers to also do more of the household tasks, as well.

In our sample, there were fifteen women in primary lesbian families who identified themselves as stay-at-home mothers. We were interested in looking at the division of labor in these families, to see how closely it resembled the unequal division typically seen in heterosexual families. The first thing we noticed about the families in which one mother was home full-time with the children was that it was not necessarily the biological mother who stayed home. Of the fifteen stay-at-home mothers, eight were the biological mothers, five were the nonbiological mothers, and two were coadoptive mothers. We then looked at the stay-at-home mothers' reports of how they allocated tasks and found an interesting pattern. As we expected, the mothers who stay at home reported that they do more of the household tasks than their employed partners.

However, the partners were more similar in how much of the childcare they each did; in fact, in six of these families (40 percent), the stay-at-home mother indicated that she and her partner shared childcare equally or that the partner did a little more of it than she did. In contrast, only four (28 percent) of them shared household tasks evenly.

Extrapolating from this group of lesbian families, we draw some preliminary conclusions. When lesbian couples have a child together and make the decision that one of them will stay home full-time to care for the child, it is slightly more likely that the biological mother, rather than the nonbiological mother, will be the one to stay home. In these families, the full-time mother does the bulk of the housework (although in only one case did a full-time mother indicate that she does all the housework). Both the full-time mother and the employed mother participate in caring for the child. In almost all cases, they are equally involved in childcare or one partner does only slightly more than the other.

We were unable to look at lesbian stepfamilies or gay couples in which one parent stayed home full-time, because very few of those families had that arrangement. In the case of both the lesbian and the gay stepfamilies, the likely reason is that their children were much older. In none of the primary gay families did one parent stay home full-time. Whether this arrangement is very uncommon among gay fathers or whether our sample was just not large enough to have included such families is something that we hope others will shed light on in the future.

Within lesbian families, then, fairly egalitarian arrangements seem to be the norm. This was the case for couples who had (or adopted) a child together, as well as for couples who brought the child into a new lesbian relationship. In terms of this sample, we should keep several things in mind. Among the group who had the child within the context of the lesbian relationship, many of the children were still under the age of three. It may be that, as children get older, the workload will become more evenly shared. Among the group that brought the child into the relationship, the average length of the lesbian relationship was only three years. Perhaps in these families, the nonbiological mother is moving slowly in terms of taking on childcare responsibilities.

Our examination of gay fathers' division of labor proved to be a bit more challenging. With the lesbian couples, we had the relatively easy task of comparing the biological mother with the nonbiological mother. Since nearly all the primary gay families had been formed through adoption, with both parents adopting together, making the decision how to divide the couples was less clear. There was no equivalent for the biological mother in these couples. Our distinction would have to be somewhat artificial. Given that, we chose to take advantage of the fact that each couple in our study had received two identical sets of questionnaires to complete, one marked "A" and one marked "B." We ultimately decided to split the couples on the basis of whether they had completed the "A" set of questionnaires or the "B" set of questionnaires. This was, obviously, an arbitrary distinction, but our interest was in looking at the pattern of how couples divide the work involved in raising a child, and maintaining a household. Given that these parents had jointly adopted a child there was no a priori assumption as to which one might be more involved in

TABLE 9.5

Division of Labor among Fathers in Adoptive Primary Gay Families

	Father A	Father B	t-Test
HOUSEKEEPING			
Mean	3.21[1]	4.41	3.19**
Standard deviation	1.18	1.06	
CHILD REARING			
Mean	3.63	4.24	2.01
Standard deviation	0.89	0.90	

NOTE: Nineteen couples were included in this analysis.

[1] 1 = I do it all; 4 = We share equally; 7 = My partner does it all; $**p \leq .01$

childcare, for example. Therefore, making an arbitrary classification system (Father "A" and Father "B") would allow us to determine whether or not these families divided the tasks evenly.

We found that there was a significant difference between the adoptive gay fathers in how they handled household tasks (see Table 9.5). These families were not strictly equal in their sharing of housework. One partner seemed to do more than the other, on average. The difference in childcare responsibilities was not as strong, although there was a tendency for the father who was more involved with the household tasks to also do more of the childcare.

Taken together, what do our results suggest about egalitarianism and gay and lesbian parents? First, there seems to be a real effort on the part of our participants to share the tasks equally, and half of them feel they do just that. In the remainder of families, the tasks are nearly equally divided, with one partner doing slightly more of the work associated with childcare and with running a house. In lesbian families, it is the biological mother who does more. It is not clear, from our sample of gay fathers, what leads one parent to be the more involved one. Among these families, there was no rigid allocation of roles, as is typically found in heterosexual families.

Communication about and Commitment to the Child

An important aspect of the relationship between parents is how they view each other's performance and ability as parents. The parents' investment in the child, their opinion of their partners' parental skills, and their degree of communication and agreement about the child make up what is called the "parental alliance." This is thought to be separate and distinct from their overall satisfaction with the relationship. Researchers (see Abidin & Brunner, 1995, for example) have hypothesized that the strength of the parental alliance is related to parenting behavior and, ultimately, to children's adjustment. We did not assess children's adjustment in this study, but we did want to examine levels of parental alliance in our families to determine their relationship to different family types or to other demographic variables.

Scores on the parental alliance measure were consistent with scores that have been reported on married heterosexual parents. Abidin and Brunner (1995), for example, reported a mean of 84 for married women and 86 for married men; mean scores for gay and lesbian parents were in that range, if not a bit higher. We were interested in examining whether the strength of the parental alliance differed by family type. We found that it did. Our analysis focused on the four groups: males versus females, and stepfamily versus primary gay or lesbian family. We did not have enough subjects in the "blended" or "other" family groups to include them in the analyses. We found that family type did make a difference in how strongly the partners felt about each other's abilities as parents (see Table 9.6). Specifically, mothers in lesbian stepfamilies (that is, those whose children were born or adopted before the lesbian relationship) showed lower levels of communication and positive feeling about their partner as parents than did all other groups (see Table 9.7). That is, in the lesbian "stepfamilies", mothers expressed more concerns about the parenting skills of their partners than did mothers in primary lesbian families. This is not entirely surprising; studies on heterosexual stepfamilies show that the first years of life in a new stepfamily are often quite stressful, and differences of opinion between the adults on how to deal with the children are common. Our research suggests that similar dynamics may be at play in lesbian stepfamilies. New stepparents obviously have less experience as parents, while their partners have been parenting for years. Not only are the new partners less experienced at parenting generally; they have no shared history with the children and are less intimately acquainted with their personalities. The partners have no shared parenting history, either, and may have very different outlooks on how to manage children. Our findings on parental involvement showed that stepmothers in lesbian stepfamilies are

TABLE 9.6

Parenting Alliance by Family Type

	Mean (SD)	Number of Subjects	F(3,320)
WOMEN			
Primary lesbian	91.7 (7.1)[b]	197	32.9***
Lesbian stepfamily	80.1 (12.5)[a]	70	
MEN			
Primary gay	88.2 (7.9)[b]	48	
Gay stepfamily	94.8 (4.6)[b]	9	

NOTE: Parenting alliance score has a theoretical range of 20–100.

Means with different superscripts differ significantly at $p < .05$ level using Spjotroll/Stoline test for unequal n's; ***$p < .001$

Groups with superscript [b] did not differ significantly from one another.

The group with superscript [a] differed significantly from the other three groups.

TABLE 9.7

Lesbian Mothers' Parenting Alliance by Family Type

	Primary Lesbian Family	Lesbian Stepfamily	t-test
Mean	91.7	80.1	9.47***
SD	(7.1)	(12.5)	
N	197	70	

NOTE: ***$p < .001$

very involved in child rearing, although as a group they have less involvement than the biological birth mothers. Taken together, the results suggest that in lesbian stepfamilies the stepmother plays an active, parental role with the children, but the partners do have more disagreements about child rearing.

It is important to keep in mind that, even though the parental alliance scores are lower in the lesbian stepfamilies than in the families that originated as lesbian families, the scores are not so low as to signify that these families were in distress. It would be interesting to compare lesbian stepfamilies with heterosexual stepfamilies on these variables. It may be that lesbian stepfamilies differ in some important ways from heterosexual stepfamilies. Given the greater participation in childcare on the part of lesbian stepmothers, it might be that more disagreements over the children arise. On the other hand, it may be that the high level of involvement on the part of the stepparents means that lesbian stepfamilies have a briefer period of adjustment, and begin functioning like a family sooner than heterosexual stepfamilies. This is an intriguing area that requires further research.

Among gay fathers, a different pattern emerged. Men in gay stepfamilies scored higher than men in primary gay families on the parenting alliance scale, although this difference was not statistically significant. (The difference between the two gay father groups was less than the difference between the two lesbian mother groups.) Men in gay stepfamilies appear to feel more positively about their partners' parenting abilities than do the men in primary gay families. We note that our sample contained very few gay father stepfamilies, and so the results involving them should be viewed with caution. Future studies can examine this apparent difference between types of gay father families.

Satisfaction with the Adult Relationship

Sharing parenting is only one aspect of couples' relationships. The adult romantic relationship itself is multifaceted. Our measure of the adult relationship consisted of an overall adjustment measure, which itself comprised four subscores. We examined the overall adjustment scores of the four groups of parents (see Table 9.8) and found, first, that the scores were comparable to scores found in studies of married heterosexual couples (Spanier, 1976, for example, reports a mean of 114.8 in his sample). We also found that one group, men in primary gay families, scored lower than all other groups on overall adjustment. Of the four groups of gay and lesbian families we looked at, the ones who were least satisfied with their adult relationships were the gay men who had had children together.

Wanting to explore this finding in more detail, we then examined each of the subscores to see whether we could determine specifically where the problems in that group were. As we have mentioned, the overall adjustment score comprises four scores (Consensus, Satisfaction, Affection, and Cohesion), each of which assesses an important, yet separate aspect of intimate adult relationships. Consensus refers to the couples' agreement on issues such as finances, career decisions, choices in how to spend free time, and so on. Satisfaction in-

TABLE 9.8

Relationship Adjustment Means by Family Type

	Mean (SD)	Number of Subjects	F(3,325)
WOMEN			
Primary lesbian	118.7 (11.5)[b]	197	4.59**
Lesbian stepfamily	118.6 (13.8)[b]	70	
MEN			
Primary gay	111.7 (12.4)[a]	48	
Gay stepfamily	120.3 (14.1)[b]	9	

NOTE: Scores are the total on the Dyadic Adjustment Scale, with a theoretical range of 0–151. **p < .01

Groups with superscript [b] did not differ significantly from one another.

The group with superscript [a] differed significantly from the other three groups.

TABLE 9.9

Relationship Variable Means by Family Type

	WOMEN		MEN		
	Primary Lesbian	Lesbian Stepfamily	Primary Gay	Gay Stepfamily	F(3,325)
Consensus	51.0 (5.5)[b]	50.5 (6.6)[b]	47.3 (5.9)[a]	51.8 (6.4)[b]	5.58***
Affection	8.8 (2.1)	8.8 (2.0)	8.4 (2.2)	9.3 (2.1)	0.73
Satisfaction	38.1 (2.9)	37.8 (3.4)	37.6 (3.0)	38.8 (3.3)	0.64
Cohesion	17.8 (2.9)[b]	18.9 (3.1)[b]	16.4 (3.2)[a]	17.4 (3.3)	6.42***

NOTE: Numbers represent score means; standard deviations are given parentheses. Means in the same row with different superscripts differ significantly at p < .05 using Least Squared Difference Test; ***p < .001.

In each row, the groups with superscript [b] did not differ significantly from one another.

The group with superscript [a] differed significantly from the other three groups.

dicates how well the couple gets along in general, and how infrequently they quarrel or argue or generally get on each other's nerves. The affection score reflects the physical dimension of the adults' relationship. Finally, cohesion concerns how often the partners engage in outside interests together, discuss ideas, and enjoy each other's company. Table 9.9 presents mean scores for each of the four groups. There were no differences among the four groups in measures of affection or satisfaction. Participants in all groups were satisfied with the physical aspect of their relationship, and all reported low rates of arguments and general disagreements. We found that two of the four areas were problematic for men in primary gay families. In consensus and cohesion, men in primary gay families scored significantly lower than parents in other groups. On consensus, they scored lower than all other groups. On cohesion, they scored lower than both lesbian mother groups.

This finding suggests that the areas of cohesion and consensus may be of particular concern for gay fathers who have a child together. These areas assess how well the couple works together, and their general agreement on how they spend their time together. It is not clear why gay fathers who have a child together would have more difficulty in this area, as opposed to lesbian mothers or fathers in gay stepfamilies. This suggests an intriguing direction for future research. It also bears repeating that fathers in primary gay families report that they are as affectionate with their partners and are as satisfied with their relationships as are the other parents in this study.

Disciplinary Techniques: How Do Gay and Lesbian Parents Discipline Their Children?

We asked subjects to report on the types of disciplinary techniques they use in a typical week with their child. We separated the responses into positive techniques (e.g. distracting, reasoning, or negotiating with the child) and negative techniques (e.g. spanking, yelling in anger, and withdrawing privileges). We did not find any significant differences among the groups of parents on their use of negative discipline techniques; all reported quite low levels of use of these methods. No group of families differed significantly from any other group in their use of negative techniques, although future studies with larger samples may find some differences.

TABLE 9.10

Use of Discipline Techniques by Family Type

| | WOMEN | | MEN | | |
	Primary Lesbian	Lesbian Stepfamily	Primary Gay	Gay Stepfamily	$F(3,308)$
Positive Discipline Techniques	14.2 (6.6)	9.4 (6.0)[b]	16.4 (6.3)[a]	8.6 (3.7)[b]	16.32***
Negative Discipline Techniques	2.3 (2.3)	3.0 (2.2)	3.1 (2.2)	1.3 (1.5)	4.01**
Total	16.5 (8.0)[c]	12.4 (7.6)[b,d]	19.5 (7.1)[a]	9.9 (4.3)[b]	11.16***

NOTE: ***$p < .001$; **$p < .01$. Means with superscript [a] differ from those with superscript [b] significantly at $p < .05$ level using Spjotroll/Stoline test for unequal n's. Means with superscript [c] differ from those with superscript [d] significantly at $p < .05$ level using Spjotroll/Stoline test for unequal n's.

TABLE 9.11

Percentage of Parents Who Do Not Spank by Family Type

WOMEN		
	Primary lesbian	86% (107)
	Lesbian stepfamily	89% (66)
	Blended family	86% (12)
MEN		
	Primary gay	95% (40)
	Gay stepfamily	100% (10)

NOTE: Includes responses of parents whose children were over two years of age.

Among the negative discipline techniques we asked about was spanking, and we wanted to look at that individually. It is well documented that, in American families, corporal punishment is a common occurrence. Straus (1994), for example, cites data from national samples showing that the majority of American parents do hit or spank their children, with overall rates being in excess of 60 percent. Our sample of gay and lesbian parents showed a very different pattern (see Table 9.11). Few parents in any group spanked their children in a typical week. The low rates of corporal punishment are remarkable in that they differ so much from the rates reported by heterosexual parents. We note that we did not include responses from parents of children younger than two in our analyses, so we could be confident that our results were not misleading because they included parents of infants. Our finding that fewer than 15 percent of our participants resort to physical punishment demonstrates, finally, one way in which gay and lesbian parents really do differ significantly from heterosexual parents in their ways of interacting with their children. Other studies comparing parents who spank with parents who do not have found that nonspanking parents are more attentive to their children, use more explanations and reasoning with them, and are more warm and affectionate toward their children (Straus, 1994).

In Chapter 2 we discussed the authoritative style of parenting, which is characterized by high levels of warmth on the one hand and high levels of demandingness on the other. Authoritative parents tend to use physical punishment infrequently and are more likely to rely on methods that are more respectful of the child, such as reasoning and discussing. As we mentioned in our earlier discussion of this parenting style, children whose parents treat them in this manner are most likely to grow up to be mature, responsible, self-confident people. Our findings suggest that most gay and lesbian parents are likely to be classified as authoritative and that this has positive implications for their children's development.

We found that fathers in primary gay families reported higher rates of overall use of discipline methods (both positive and negative) than did fathers in gay stepfamilies or mothers in lesbian stepfamilies. Mothers in primary lesbian families reported more use of discipline measures in a typical week than did mothers in lesbian stepfamilies.

We also found low to moderate negative correlations between the oldest child's age and the parents' use of different discipline techniques (see Table 9.12). This suggests that, as children get older, their parents use fewer disciplinary tactics. It is important to bear this finding in mind, for in this sample

TABLE 9.12

Correlations between Oldest Child's Age and Use of Disciplinary Techniques

	Positive Discipline	Negative Discipline	Total
Mothers	−.26*	.12*	−.18*
Fathers	−.37*	.07	−.33*

NOTE: *$p < .05$

the children of the lesbian stepfamilies were, on average, five years older than the children in the primary lesbian families. It could be that the difference in the children's ages accounts for the difference in use of disciplinary measures between the two types of lesbian families.

[10]

Conclusion

There are two questions we wish to address in concluding our study and our book. The first is, How are gay and lesbian families doing in the United States today? The second, more specific, question is, What are the most promising future directions for psychological research on these families?

How Well Are Gay and Lesbian Parents Functioning?

The participants of this study allowed us to look inside their families to see how they are functioning. They also allowed us to see how they interact with the larger community and how the community responds to them. In general, we found that most of the problem areas, whether actual or anticipated, came not from within the families but from the communities.

According to our results, gay- and lesbian-headed families are functioning very well. As a group, they scored as well as, or better than, heterosexual couples on measures of relationship adjustment and satisfaction, allocation of tasks related to child rearing and housekeeping, and communication about their children. Gay and lesbian parents put a high premium on teaching their children to respect others and to value diversity. Few of them use physical punishment with their children. This particular sample was a well-educated, well-paid group of parents, and this certainly contributes to their overall well-being.

The primary difficulties were found outside the families. Most of the lesbian mothers, and a sizable minority of gay fathers, faced opposition from their own families about becoming parents. By far the most common concern of these parents was that their children would be teased or treated unkindly by others because of the parent's sexual orientation. Clearly, a lack of support from people and institutions outside the family is something that many gay and lesbian parents must face. Their approach to the outside world seems to be to present themselves as a family deserving of recognition and respect. Most of the families were living openly as gay or lesbian families within their communities by coming out to their children's teachers, doctors, or friends' parents. This suggests that one way that gay and lesbian parents deal with anticipated disapproval from others is by meeting it head on. They make efforts to find the most supportive and accepting individuals and institutions they can for their children, including doctors and teachers, and they make a point of educating others.

While only a minority of the subjects reported any extremely negative experiences, these events did still occur. There is by no means universal acceptance of these parents or their families.

The children of those parents in this sample who came out before having children are still quite young. It may be that, as the children get older, their gay and lesbian parents will face issues they had not anticipated. Future studies may wish to address this question. Differences among the groups of gay and lesbian parents are certainly worthy of further exploration, as well.

In terms of the characteristics that go along with being effective parents, as we discussed in Chapter 2, the evidence from our study and the many other studies that have been done on gay- and lesbian-headed families shows that gay men and lesbians make very effective parents. Our study, and the other studies we have reviewed, found that gay and lesbian parents show strengths in the security of attachment to their children; in their parenting styles, including how they discipline their children; in the quality of their own couple relationships; and in how they share the work associated with raising children and running a household.

Future Directions for Research

The Heterogeneous Population of Gay and Lesbian Parents

We found that gay men and lesbians take different routes to parenthood and have different experiences along the way. Lesbians who become mothers after coming out usually choose to bear their own biological children. The majority of them face resistance, at least initially, from their own families.

It is not uncommon for them to worry that their employment may be affected by their plans to have a child. Gay men who have children after coming out almost always choose to adopt their children. Most of them do not encounter any disapproval from their own families, and they neither anticipate nor experience any employment-related problems as they begin their families. Parents who have children within a heterosexual relationship and then form a lesbian or gay stepfamily face a different set of issues, including fear of losing custody and anxiety about establishing a new family.

Researchers should be aware of the diverse subgroups of gay and lesbian parents and should take into account their different life experiences. It is not sufficient to obtain a sample of dissimilar families who have only one thing in common—the sexual orientation of the parents. The different pathways that people took to parenthood continue to impact their parenting and their children. We will miss what is unique about different kinds of families if we lump them all together.

Gay Fathers

The majority of research on gay and lesbian parents has actually been conducted on lesbian mothers. Gay fathers have been understudied, perhaps, in part, because there are fewer of them. Our study was open to both gay and lesbian parents, and we solicited participants from groups, bulletin boards, and so forth that appealed to both sexes. Still, most of our respondents were lesbian mothers. Even if there are fewer gay fathers than lesbian mothers, their concerns need to be addressed in the literature. We hope that more researchers will focus on this group of parents and their children in the future.

Community Support

We found, as we stated before, that social support is an issue in one way or another for many gay and lesbian families. They often encounter a lack of support for their plans to become parents, and they worry about how others will treat their children. Since the area of support from people outside one's own immediate family is such a crucial one, we hope that future research will devote itself to this topic. We believe that gay and lesbian parents who have more support from others-more acceptance from their own families, more community support in the way of accepting schools for their children, a diverse neighborhood where there are other gay- or lesbian-headed families, and an active gay and lesbian community-will experience less stress and be more effective parents than those gay and lesbian parents who lack these resources. We look forward to studies that examine these variables.

One rapidly changing area of social support is the legal system. More states are allowing second-parent adoptions than ever before, and this public validation of gay and lesbian families has many effects. Some of the parents in our study remarked about the uneasiness they felt regarding their lack of a legal tie to their children. We suspect that having the ability to procure a second-parent adoption benefits gay and lesbian families psychologically, as well as in other ways. We would be interested in seeing studies that examine the impact of legal recognition of gay and lesbian families, both on parents and on children.

Use of the Right Control Group

As we have noted, a common research design is to compare children of gays or lesbians to children of heterosexual parents. This strategy is not without merit. However, it is important that the "right" control group be used in each study. For example, often two groups of children of divorced parents are studied: one group that is living with their heterosexual mothers and one group that is living with their lesbian mothers. In most of the studies with this design that we discussed, most of the lesbian mothers had new partners, while most of the heterosexual mothers did not. This fact obviously presents a confound, in that there is not only one difference between the two groups of children-the sexual orientation of their mothers-but also a second difference, the presence of a stepparent. It is important not to muddy the waters in this manner. Researchers must be careful to disentangle the effects of divorce from the effects of the forming of a stepfamily.

We use this example purposely, for children living in lesbian stepfamilies may well differ from children living in heterosexual stepfamilies. Our results found that lesbian stepmothers are very involved in their stepchildren's lives. This heightened involvement may mean that lesbian stepfamilies do not go through the same type of adjustment that heterosexual families go through. They may experience a briefer transition time, because of the increase in the child-stepmother involvement. On the other hand, the more active participation of a lesbian stepmother may mean that there is more conflict early on in the family, as the stepmother becomes a more active participant in family life. This is a very fruitful area for further research, and it is important that the appropriate control group of heterosexual stepfamilies be used so that accurate comparisons can be made.

Other Research Designs

Recently, researchers have begun to study gay and lesbian families using methods other than self-report, as we have used. Studies that include assessments from teachers, psychologists, and other professionals are beginning to be made, and this is a positive move. Researchers are also taking on longitudinal projects, in which the same group of families is followed over the course of several years. This, also, is a much-needed advance in the study of gay and lesbian families.

The Internet is a powerful tool for researchers interested in studying these families. Historically, it has been difficult, if not impossible, to find participants who live outside metropolitan areas and who are not involved in some sort of parenting groups. The availability of the many Web sites, list serves, and chat rooms for gay and lesbian parents means that parents who might otherwise be inaccessible to researchers can now be contacted. This is an exciting development for researchers, who now have an opportunity to include a more diverse, representative sample of gay and lesbian parents.

The Internet also offers the benefit of anonymity. In order to preserve our subjects' confidentiality, we promised to destroy our record of their mailing address once we had sent them the questionnaires. Only a few of our subjects asked about this or expressed any concern; in fact, several of our participants stated that they would be willing to be identified by name in any publications that arose from the project. For those who were worried about anonymity, however, the chance to participate in a study without being publicly identified was an opportunity they eagerly embraced.

Positive Influences on Children of Gay and Lesbian Parents

Parents in our study strongly believed that their children would benefit from having gay or lesbian parents, that they would be more accepting of diversity and tolerant of other people. While there is some evidence to suggest that this is true of children raised by gay or lesbian parents, it has not yet been examined systematically. Some of our respondents indicated that they felt their children would be less constrained by gender-role stereotypes. Some lesbian mothers felt their sons and daughters would grow to be more respectful of women. Whether these effects are wishful thinking or reflect actual influences upon children of gays and lesbians remains to be seen.

The focus of much of the research so far has been on potential problems. The time is now at hand to assess potential advantages. For example, are children of gays and lesbians more emotionally or socially mature as a result of having to deal with homophobia? Are they more open with their parents in discussions of sexuality, since their parents must have broached the topic themselves in talking about their own sexual orientation? Are they more likely to grow up and be highly involved parents themselves?

These questions have yet to be asked. We look forward to research that focuses on the strengths and positive outcomes of these remarkable families.

References

Abindin, R. R., & Brunner, J. F. (1995). Development of a parenting alliance inventory. *Journal of Clinical Child Psychology*, 24 (1), 31–40.

Ainsworth, M. D. S., Blehar, M., Waters, E., & Wall, S. (1978). *Patterns of attachment*. Hillsdale, NJ: Erlbaum.

Bailey, J. M., & Pillard, R. C. (1991). A genetic study of male sexual orientation. *Archives of General Psychiatry*, 48, 1089–1096.

Bailey, J. M., Bobrow, D., Wolfe, M., & Mikach, S. (1995). Sexual orientation of adults sons of gay fathers. *Developmental Psychology*, 31(1), 124–129.

Baumrind, D. (1967). Child care practices anteceding three patterns of preschool behavior. *Genetic Psychology Monographs*, 75, 43–88.

Baumrind, D. (1971). Current patterns of parental authority. *Developmental Psychology Monograph*, 4 (1, pt. 2), 1-103.

Baumrind, D. (1991). The influence of parenting style on adolescent competence and substance use. *Journal of Early Adolescence*, 11, 56–95.

Baumrind, D., & Black, A. E. (1967). Socialization practices associated with dimensions of competence in preschool boys and girls. *Child Development*, 38, 291–327.

Belsky, J. (1984). The determinants of parenting: A process model. *Child Development*, 55(1), 83–96.

Belsky, J., Rovine, M., & Taylor, D. G. (1984). The Pennsylvania infant and family development project: III. The origins of individual differences in infant-mother attachment: Maternal and infant contributions. *Child Development*, 55, 718–728.

Bem, S. L. (1974). The measurement of psychological androgyny. *Journal of Consulting and Clinical Psychology*, 42, 155–162.

Bem, S. L. (1977). On the utility of alternative procedures for assessing psychological androgyny. *Journal of Consulting and Clinical Psychology*, 45, 196–205.

Benson, P. L., Sharma, A. R., & Roehlkepartain, E. C. (1994). *Growing up adopted: A portrait of adolescents and their family.* Minneapolis: Search Institute.

Bernstein, A. C. (1994). *The flight of the stork: What children think (and when) about sex and family building.* Indianapolis, IN: Perspectives Press.

Bigner, J. J., & Jacobsen, R. B. (1989). Parenting behaviors of homosexual and heterosexual fathers. *Journal of Homosexuality*, 18(1–2), 173–186.

Bigner, J. J., & Jacobson, R. (1992). Adult responses to child behavior and attitudes toward fathering: Gay and nongay fathers. *Journal of Homosexuality*, 23(3), 99–112.

Block, J. (1971). *Lives through time*. Berkeley, CA: Bancroft Books.

Block, J., Block, J., & Morrison, A. (1981). Parental agreement-disagreement on child rearing orientations and gender-related personality correlates in children. *Child Development*, 52, 965–974.

Blumstein, P., & Schwartz, P. (1983). *American couples*. New York: William Morrow.

Boldizar, J. P. (1991). Assessing sex typing and androgyny in children: The children's sex role inventory. *Developmental Psychology*, 27, 505–515.

Bowlby, J. (1969). Attachment and Loss: Vol. 1, Attachment. New York: Basic Books.

Bowlby, J. (1973). Attachment and Loss: Vol. 2, Separation. New York: Basic Books.

Bozett, F. W. (1980). Gay fathers: How and why they disclose their homosexuality to their children. *Family Relations*, 29, 173–179.

Bozett, F. W. (1981). Gay fathers: Evolution of the gay father identity. *American Journal of Orthopsychiatry*, 51, 552–559.

Brand, E., Clingempeel, W. E., & Bowen-Woodward, K. (1988). Family relationships and children's psychological adjustment in stepmother and stepfather families: Findings and conclusions from the Philadelphia Stepfamily Research Project. In E. M. Hetherington & J. D. Arasteh (Eds.), *Impact of divorce, single parenting, and stepparenting on children* (pp. 299–324). Hillsdale, NJ: Erlbaum.

Bretherton, I. (1990). Open communication and internal working models: Their role in the development of attachment relationships. In R. A. Thompson (Ed.), *Nebraska Symposium on Motivation: Vol. 36. Socioemotional development* (pp. 57–113). Lincoln, NE: University of Nebraska Press.

Bronfenbrenner, U. (1979). *The ecology of human development*. Cambridge, MA: Harvard University Press.

Bronfenbrenner, U. (1989). Ecological systems theory. In R. Vasta (Ed.), *Annals of child development: Vol. 6. Six theories of child development: revised formulations and current issues*. Greenwich, CT: JAI Press.

Brodzinsky, D., Smith, D., & Brodzinsky, A. (1998). *Children's adjustment to adoption: Developmental and clinical issues*. Thousand Oaks, CA: Sage Publications.

Buchanan, C. M., Maccoby, E. E., & Dornbusch, S. M. (1991). Caught between parents: Adolescents' experience in divorced homes. *Child Development*, 62, 1008–1029.

Buehler, C. A., Krishnakumar, A., Stone, G., Gerard, J., & Pemberton, S. (1997). Interparental conflict and youth problem behaviors: A meta-analysis. *Journal of Child and Family Studies*, 6, 233–247.

Chadwick, B., & Heaton, T. B. (Eds.). (1999). *Statistical handbook on the American family*. Phoenix, AZ: Oryx Press.

Chan, R. W., Brooks, R. S., Raboy, B., & Patterson, C. J. (1998). Division of labor among lesbian and heterosexual parents:

Associations with children's adjustment. *Journal of Family Psychology*, 12(3), 402–419.

Cowan, C. P., & Cowan, P. A. (1992). *When partners become parents: The big life change for couples.* New York: Basic Books.

Cox, M. J., Owen, M. T., Henderson, V. K., & Lewis, J. M. (1989). Marriage, adult adjustment, and early parenting. *Child Development*, 60, 1015–1024.

Deal, J. E., Hagan, M. S., & Anderson, E. R. (1992). The marital relationship in remarried families. In E. M. Hetherington & W. G Clingempeel (Eds.), *Coping with marital transitions: A family systems perspective. Monographs of the Society for Research in Child Development*, serial no. 227, 57 (2–3), pp. 73–93.

Deevey, S. (1989). When mom or dad comes out: Helping adolescents cope with homophobia. *Journal of Psychosocial Nursing and Mental Health Services*, 27, 857–865.

Denham, S. A., Renwick, S. M., & Holt, R. (1991). Working and playing together: Prediction of preschool social-emotional competence from mother-child interaction. *Child Development*, 62, 242–249.

DiLapi, E. M. (1989). Lesbian mothers and the motherhood hierarchy. In F. W. Bozett (Ed.), *Homosexuality and the family*. New York: Harrington Park Press.

Dunkel-Schetter, C., Sagrestano, L. M., Feldman, P., & Killingsworth, C. (1996). Social support and pregnancy. In G. R. Pierce, B. R. Sarason, & I. G. Sarason (Eds.), *Handbook of social support and the family* (pp. 375–412). New York: Plenum Press.

Elicker, J., Englund, M., & Sroufe, L. A. (1992). Predicting peer competence and peer relationships in childhood from early parent-child relationships. In R. D. Parke & G. W. Ladd (Eds.), *Family-peer relationships: Modes of linkage* (pp. 77–106). Hillsdale, NJ: Erlbaum.

Fauber, R., Forehand, R., Thomas, A., & Wierson, M. (1990). A mediational model of the impact of marital conflict on adolescent adjustment in intact and divorced families. *Child Development*, 61, 1112–1123.

Flaks, D. K., Ficher, I., Masterpasqua, F., & Joseph, G. (1995). Lesbians choosing motherhood: A comparative study of lesbian and heterosexual parents and their children. *Developmental Psychology*, 33(1), 105–114.

Gartrell, N., Banks, A., Hamilton, J., Reed, N., Bishop, H., & Rodas, C. (1999). The national lesbian family study: 2. Interviews with mothers of toddlers. *American Journal of Orthopsychiatry*, 69(3), 362–369.

Gartrell, N., Banks, A., Reed, N., Hamilton, J., Rodas, C., & Deck, A. (2000). The national lesbian family study: 3. Interviews with mothers of five-year-olds. *American Journal of Orthopsychiatry*, 70(4), 542–548.

Gartrell, N., Hamilton, J., Banks, A., Mosbacher, D., Reed, N., Sparks, C. H., & Bishop, H. (1996). The national lesbian family study: 1. Interviews with prospective mothers. *American Journal of Orthopsychiatry*, 66(2), 272–281.

Gershon, T. D., Tschann, J. M., & Jemerin, J. M. (1999). Stigmatization, self-esteem, and coping among the adolescent children of lesbian mothers. *Journal of Adolescent Health*, 24, 437–445.

Golombok, S. (1999). New family forms: Children raised in solo mother families, lesbian mother families, and in families created by assisted reproduction. In L. Balter & C. S. Tamis-LeMonda (Eds.), *Child psychology: A handbook of contemporary issues* (pp. 429–446). Philadelphia: Psychology Press.

Golombok, S., Cook, R., Bish, A., & Murray, C. (1995). Families created by the new reproductive technologies: Quality of parenting and social and emotional development of the children. *Child Development*, 66, 285–298.

Golombok, S., Spencer, A., and Rutter, M. (1983). Children in lesbian and single-parent households: Psychosexual and psychiatric appraisal. *Journal of Child Psychology and Psychiatry*, 24(40), 551–572.

Golombok, S., Tasker, F., & Murray, C. (1997). Children raised in fatherless families from infancy: Family relationships and the socioemotional development of children of lesbian and single heterosexual mothers. *Journal of Child Psychology and Psychiatry*, 38(7), 783–791.

Gottman, J. S. (1990). Children of gay and lesbian parents. In F. W.Bozett & M. B.Sussman (Eds.), *Homosexuality and family relations* (pp. 177–196). New York: Harrington Park Press.

Green, R. (1978). Sexual identity of 37 children raised by homosexual or transsexual parents. *American Journal of Psychiatry*, 135(6), 692–697.

Green, R., Mandel, J. B., Hotvedt, M. E., Gray, J., & Smith, L. (1986). Lesbian mothers and their children: A comparison with solo parent heterosexual mothers and their children. *Archives of Sexual Behavior*, 15, 167–184.

Grotevant, H. D., & McRoy, R. G. (1998). *Openness in adoption: Exploring family connections*. New York: Sage.

Grych, J. H., Fincham, F. D., Jouriles, E. N., & McDonald, R. (2000). Interparental conflict and child adjustment: Testing the mediational role of appraisals in the cognitive-contextual framework. *Child Development*, 71(6), 1648–1661.

Hagan, M. S., Hollier, E. A., O'Connor, T. G., & Eisenberg, M. (1992). Parent-child relationships in nondivorced, divorced single-mother, and remarried families. In E. M. Hetherington & W. G. Clingempeel (Eds.), *Coping with marital transitions: A family systems perspective. Monographs of the Society for Research in Child Development*, serial no. 227, 57(2–3), pp. 94–148.

Hand, S. I. (1991). The lesbian parenting couple. Unpublished Ph.D.diss., Professional School of Psychology, San Francisco.

Harris, M. B., & Turner, P. H. (1986). Gay and lesbian parents. *Journal of Homosexuality*, 12(2), 101–113

Hetherington, E. M (1993). An overview of the Virginia Longitudinal Study of Divorce and Remarriage: A focus on early adolescence. *Journal of Family Psychology*, 7, 39–56.

Hetherington, E. M., & Clingempeel, W. G. (Eds.) (1992). *Coping with marital transitions: A family systems perspective. Monographs of the Society for Research in Child Development*, serial no. 227, 57(2–3).

Hetherington, E. M., Cox, M. J., & Cox, R. (1985). Long-term effects of divorce and remarriage on the adjustment of children. *Journal of the American Academy of Child and Adolescent Psychiatry*, 24, 518–530.

Hochschild, A. R. (1989). *The second shift: Working parents and the revolution at home*. New York: Viking Penguin.

Hoeffer, B. (1981). Children's acquisition of sex-role behavior in lesbian mothers. *American Journal of Orthopsychiatry*, 51(3), 536–544.

Holden, G. W., & Zambarano, R. J. (1992). Passing the rod: Similarities between parents and their young children in orientations toward physical punishment. In I. E. Seigel, A. V. McGillicuddy-DeLise, & J. J. Goodnow, (Eds.), *Parental belief systems: The psychological consequences for children* (2d ed., pp. 143–172). Hillsdale, NJ: Erlbaum.

Howes, P., & Markman, H. J (1989). Marital quality and child functioning: A longitudinal investigation. *Child Development*, 60, 1044–1051.

Huggins, S. L. (1989). A comparative study of self-esteem of adolescent children of divorced lesbian mothers and divorced heterosexual mothers. In F. W. Bozett (Ed.), *Homosexuality and the family* (pp. 123–135). New York: Harrington Park Press.

Kirkpatrick, M., Smith, C., & Roy, R. (1981). Lesbian mothers and their children: A comparative survey. *American Journal of Orthopsychiatry*, 51(3), 545–551.

Kurdek, L. (1993). The allocation of household labor in gay, lesbian, and heterosexual married couples. *Journal of Social Issues*, 49, 127–139.

Kweskin, S. L., & Cook, A. S. (1982). Heterosexual and homosexual mothers' self-described sex-role behavior and ideal sex-role behavior in children. *Sex Roles*, 8(9), 967–975.

Lamborn, S. D., Mounts, N. S., Steinberg, L., & Dornbusch, S. M. (1991). Patterns of competence and adjustment among adolescents from authoritative, authoritarian, indulgent, and neglectful families. *Child Development*, 62, 1049–1065.

Lewin, E. (1984). Lesbianism and motherhood: Implications for child custody. In T. Darty & S. Potter (Eds.), *Women identified women* (pp. 163–183). Palo Alto, CA: Mayfield.

Lott-Whitehead, L., & Tully, C. (1992). The family of lesbian mothers. *Smith College Studies in Social Work, 63*, 265–280.

Lyons, T. A. (1983). Lesbian mothers' custody fear. *Women and Therapy*, 2, 231–240.

Mahlstedt, P. E., & Greenfield, D. (1989). Assisted reproductive technology with donor gametes: The need for patient preparation. *Fertility and Sterility*, 52, 908–914.

Main, M., Kaplan, N., & Cassidy, J. (1985). Security in infancy, childhood, and adulthood: A move to the level of representation. In I. Bretheron & E. Waters (Eds.), *Growing point of attachment theory and research. Monographs of the Society for Research in Child Development*, 50(1–2), serial no. 209), 66–104.

McHale, S. M., & Crouter, A. C. (1992). You can't always get what you want: Incongruence between sex-role attitudes and family work roles and its implications for marriage. *Journal of Marriage and the Family*, 54, 536–547.

McPherson, D. (1993). Gay parenting couples: Parenting arrangements, arrangement satisfaction, and relationship satisfaction. Unpublished Ph.D. diss., Pacific Graduate School of Psychology, Palo Alto, CA.

Melina, L. (1989). *Making sense of adoption*. New York: Harper & Row.

Miller, B. (1979). Gay fathers and their children. Family Coordinator, 28(4), 544–552.

Miller, J. A., Jacobsen, R. B., & Bigner, J. J. (1981). The child's home environment for lesbian vs. heterosexual mothers: A neglected area of research. *Journal of Homosexuality*, 7(1), 49–56.

Mitchell, V. (1998). The birds, the bees . . . and the sperm banks: How lesbian mothers talk with their children about sex and reproduction. *American Journal of Orthopsychiatry*, 68(3), 400–409.

Nachtigall, R. D. (1993). Secrecy: An unresolved issue in the practice of donor insemination. *American Journal of Obstetrics and Gynecology*, 168, 1846–1851.

Pagelow, M. D. (1980). Heterosexual and lesbian single mothers: A comparison of problems, coping, and solutions. *Journal of Homosexuality*, 5(3), 189–204.

Patterson, C. J. (1994). Children of the lesbian baby boom: Behavioral adjustment, self-concepts, and sex role identity. In B. Green & G. Herek (Eds.), *Lesbian and gay psychology & theory, research, and clinical applications* (pp. 156–175). Thousand Oaks, CA: Sage.

Patterson, C. J. (1995a). Families of the lesbian baby boom: Parents' division of labor and children's adjustment. *Developmental Psychology*, 31(1), 115–123.

Patterson, C. J. (1995b). Lesbian and gay parenthood. In M. H. Bornstein (Ed.), *Handbook of parenting* (pp. 255–274). Mahwah, NJ: Erlbaum.

Patterson, C. J. (1995c). Lesbian mothers, gay fathers, and their children. In A. R. D'Augelli & C. J. Patterson (Eds.), *Lesbian, gay and bisexual identities across the lifespan* (pp. 262–290). New York: Oxford University Press.

Pianta, R. C., Sroufe, L. A., & Egeland, B. (1989). Continuity and discontinuity in maternal sensitivity at 6, 24, and 42 months in a high-risk sample. *Child Development*, 60, 481–487.

Pruett, K. D. (1992). Strange bedfellows? Reproductive technology and child development. *Infant Mental Health Journal*, 13(4), 312–318.

Pulkkinen, L. (1982). Self-control and continuity from childhood to late adolescence. In P. B. Baltes & O. G. Brim (Eds.), *Life-span development and behavior* (Vol. 4, pp. 63–105). New York: Academic Press.

Radin, N. (1981). The role of the father in cognitive, academic, and intellectual development. In M. E. Lamb (Ed.), *The role of the father in child development* (pp. 379–427). New York: Wiley.

Rand, C., Graham, D. L. R., & Rawlings, E. I. (1982). Psychological health and factors the court seeks to control in lesbian mothers custody trials. *Journal of Homosexuality*, 8(1), 27–39.

Ricketts, W., & Achtenberg, R. (1990). Adoption and foster parenting for lesbians and gay men: Creating new traditions in family. In F. W. Bozett & M. B. Sussman (Eds.), *Homosexuality and family relations*, (pp. 83–118). New York: Harrington Park Press.

Saffron, L. (1998). Raising children in an age of diversity: Advantages of having a lesbian mother. *Journal of Lesbian Studies*, 2(4), 35–47.

Savage, D. (2001). Role Reversal. *New York Times Magazine*, March 11, p. 104.

Shulman, S., Elicker, J., & Sroufe, A. (1994). Stages of friendship growth in preadolescents as related to attachment history. *Journal of Social and Personal Relationships*, 11, 341–361.

Simon, R., Altstein, H., & Melli, M. S. (1994). *The case for transracial adoption*. Washington, DC: American University Press.

Simons, R. L., & Johnson, C. (1996). The impact of marital and social network support on quality of parenting. In G. R. Pierce, B. R. Sarason, & I. G. Sarason (Eds.), *Handbook of social support and the family* (pp. 269–287). New York: Plenum Press.

Singer, L., Brodzinsky, D., Ramsay, D., Steir, M., & Waters, E. (1985). Mother-infant attachment in adoptive families. *Child Development*, 56, 1543–1551.

Snowden, R. (1990). The family and artificial reproduction. In D. Bromham, M. Dalton, & J. Jackson (Eds.), *Philosophical ethics in reproductive medicine* (pp. 70–185). Manchester, England: Manchester University Press.

Spanier, G. B. (1976). Measuring dyadic adjustment: New scales for assessing the quality of marriage and similar dyads. *Journal of Marriage and the Family*, 38(1), 15–28.

Steinberg, L. D., Lamborn, S. D., Dornbusch, S. M., & Darling, N. (1992). Impact of parenting practices on adolescent achievement: Authoritative parenting, school involvement, and encouragement to succeed. *Child Development, 63*, 1266–1282.

Stiglitz, E. (1990). Caught between two worlds: The impact of a child on a lesbian couple's relationship. *Women and Therapy,* 10(1–2), 99–116.

Straus, M. A. (1994). *Beating the devil out of them: Corporal punishment in American families.* New York: Lexington Books.

Sullivan, M. (1996). Rozzie & Harriet? Gender and family patterns of lesbian coparents. *Gender & Society,* 10(6), 747–767.

Tasker, F. L., & Golombok, S. (1997). *Growing up in a lesbian family: Effects on child development.* New York: Guilford Press.

Tasker, F. L. & Golombok, S. (1998). The role of co-mothers in planned lesbian-led families. *Journal of Lesbian Studies,* 2(4), 49–68.

Taylor, M. C., & Hall, J. A. (1982). Psychological androgyny: Theories, methods, and conclusions. *Psychological Bulletin, 9,* 347–366.

Turner, P. H., Scadden, L., & Harris, M. B. (1990). Parenting in gay and lesbian families. *Journal of Gay and Lesbian Psychotherapy,* 1(3), 55–66.

Updegraff, K. A., McHale, S. M., & Crouter, A. C. (1996). Gender roles in marriage: What do they mean for girls' and boys' school achievement? *Journal of Youth and Adolescence,* 25(1), 73–92.

Vercollone, C. F., Moss, H., & Moss, R. (1997). *Helping the stork: The choices and challenges of donor insemination.* New York: Macmillan.

Verhulst, F. C., & Versluis-Den Bieman, H. J. (1995). Developmental course of problem behaviors in adolescent adoptees. *Journal of the American Academy of Child and Adolescent Psychiatry, 34,* 151–159.

Wallerstein, J. S., & Corbin, S. B. (1989). Daughters of divorce: Report from a ten-year follow-up. *American Journal of Orthopsychiatry, 59,* 593–604.

Wallerstein, J., Lewis, J., & Blakeslee, S. (2000). *The unexpected legacy of divorce.* New York: Hyperion Books.

Wierzbicki, M. (1993). Psychological adjustment of adoptees: A meta-analysis. *Journal of Clinical Child Psychology,* 22, 447–454.

Wright, J. M. (1998). *Lesbian stepfamilies: An ethnography of love.* New York: Harrington Park Press.

Zuger, B. (1989). Homosexuality in families of boys with early effeminate behavior: An epidemiological study. *Archives of Sexual Behavior,* 18(2), 155–166.

Index

About the Authors

SUZANNE M. JOHNSON is Associate Professor of Psychology at Dowling College. ELIZABETH O'CONNOR has taught as an adjunct faculty member in social and developmental psychology at Dowling College and St. Joseph's College, in the psychology and the education departments.